I Believe

The Story of One Jewish Life

By
Leibel (Leo) Zisman

GJCF

Published by GJCF
Copyright © 2011, 2014 by Myrna Zisman

The publisher wishes to express gratitude to the United States Holocaust Memorial Museum for the use of their photo archives.

ISBN 1-886587-18-3
Printed in the United States
First Edition 2011
Second Edition 2014

The GJCF preserves the legacies of institutions and individuals that have built and advanced Jewish life. For more info: E-mail mylegacy@gjcf.net

Do not fear sudden terror or the
holocaust of the evil when it comes.[1]

Plan a conspiracy, and it will be annulled.
Speak your piece, but it shall not stand, for God is with us.[2]

[God has promised us:]
"Even until your old age, I remain unchanged.
Even until you turn gray, I shall endure.
I created you, and I shall carry you.
I shall endure and rescue you." [3]

Concluding verses of Jewish Daily Prayers

---

[1] Proverbs 3:25.
[2] Isaiah 8:10.
[3] Isaiah 46:4.

This book is dedicated to:

My father, Shraga Feivel Zisman
My mother, Leba Bluma (nee Raskin) Zisman
My sister, Tzivia Zisman, and
My little brother, Chaim Yisroel Zisman

These innocent people perished
at the hands of the Nazis.
May their memory always burn bright
and be forever blessed.

TABLE OF CONTENTS

EDITOR'S NOTE

For those readers unfamiliar with certain Jewish customs, personages and Hebrew references, explanations have been provided in the footnotes.

Additional information and details of potential use to researchers or genealogists have been included in the Appendix.

I Believe

The Story of One Jewish Life

PUBLISHER'S FOREWORD

Leibel Zisman was a familiar figure in my childhood. I would see him every Yom Kippur and Simchat Torah at 770 Eastern Parkway, the central Chabad Synagogue, coming to celebrate these special days with the Lubavitcher Rebbe. He and his dear wife, Myrna, would attend weddings and various celebrations in my community. He was a friend of my father, Gershon Jacobson, though it was only after my father passed away that we developed a real friendship and a mutual kinship.

We would meet from time to time, intending a short get-together, and instead ending up in a marathon discussion – what chassidim call a *farbrengen* – speaking about everything from God to politics, the Rebbes, the miracles of life, memories of times gone by. For hours on end we would talk, crying and laughing, and sometimes both at once.

Leibel would regale me with some of his "wilder" exploits, and just as seamlessly share the memories of his father and mother. He would enter another zone when speaking about the two Lubavitcher Rebbes to whom he had been attached.

I discovered that Leibel was a complex man, full of paradoxes. He was a person who was both a survivor of the harshest possible circumstances, which must have hardened him in so many ways, as well as a very warm, gentle and kind human being. In many ways, he embodied for me – very much like my father – the seemingly impossible contrasts lived by the generation of Holocaust survivors, and indeed, by the Jewish people as a whole. On the one hand, he possessed an extraordinary toughness and fearlessness shaped by witnessing the cruelty of existence. But on the other hand, he was a deeply sensitive and compassionate man.

This paradoxical amalgamation no doubt reflects the strange nature of *ud mutzal m'aish*, a burning ember which remains standing, smoldering, after a disastrous fire. Yes, indeed, after the Shoah, Leibel was a living, breathing, smoldering ember – scorched and darkened by unspeakable loss and pain, left for dead, but very much alive, full of hidden fire and passion, waiting for a bit of fresh air to fan the hidden sparks and bring the soul to life.

From this background of warring conflicts, Leibel emerged as a man of dignity and aplomb, reflecting life in its entirety – both the darkness and the light, the cynicism and the gravitas. At times, Leibel could be ferocious. At other times, he was gentle like a lamb.

I often felt that, throughout his life, Leibel wavered – probably unconsciously – between these two poles: his deep faith and vulnerability, and at the same time, his savvy and toughness, which (I was sure) were there to protect the gentle Leibel from the predators of the world.

Above all, I saw in Leibel a profound faith – a simple, innocent, unconditional belief in Divine Providence, in the blessings and promises of the Rebbes, in the legacy that his beloved parents left him. Whenever Leibel would speak of the Rebbe, without fail, his eyes would well up. Whenever he would speak about his father's dedication to the previous Rebbe and to other Jews, his words would radiate warmth, so much that they could melt a stone. Whenever he spoke about his miraculous survival, I felt the sense of his infinite gratitude to God for His blessings. And whenever he even mentioned his older brother, Berel, who survived with Leibel and protected him over the years, I could see before my eyes the little Leibel, the innocent boy, ripped away from his family and home, growing up in a harsh world, but blessed with an older brother who watched over and nurtured him.

No wonder. As I quickly learned, Leibel had very good "genes." He was the product of illustrious parents and grandparents, who traced their connection seven generations back to the Alter Rebbe, the founder of the Chabad Movement. Genes like that do not get extinguished in fires and in floods, even if they are challenged to emerge in a narcissistic universe.

Meeting Leibel – and hearing his fascinating life story, the miracles, the many events orchestrated by Divine Providence – gave birth to the idea of publishing a book about Leibel's astonishing life.

To get it going – fully cognizant of the initial challenges of getting any project underway – I suggested that Leibel tell his story to my son, Menachem Mendel, an excellent writer and talented soul, and that the telling should be recorded and then transcribed. We would then have a document that could be reviewed, amended, edited and ultimately turned into a book.

And so a life, confined to one man's memories, began to find its way to tangible paper.

After their initial meeting, Mendel and Leibel bonded. Mendel would visit Leibel weekly, and they would record session after session, which slowly grew to total several hundred pages of transcripts. Mendel would often come home filled with emotion, relating Leibel's amazing stories, the dangers, the risks, the abyss, the miraculous rescues.

Five years passed – it took five years to bring this work to fruition. *I Believe* was published, and the first edition quickly sold out.

So with a deep measure of joy and an even deeper measure of awe and humility, I am honored to present to you the second edition of *I Believe*, the story of one "smoldering ember," Leibel Zisman. Unfortunately, this second edition is going to print after Leibel's untimely passing.

I feel honored to have known Leibel, and to have helped facilitate the publishing of this special book – a testimony of one man's deep faith.

It may be the faith of one man, but it has the power to impact many. Before he passed away, Leibel traveled the world, speaking to students and audiences from all walks of life. It is not exaggeration to say that his passion and faith changed lives. But that is the power of a "smoldering ember" speaking.

My sincere hope is that all those who pick up this book will come away with deep inspiration and a newfound hope and faith in God, as they read about Leibel's idyllic childhood in a Jewish haven, about the dark day when he was taken to the camps, about his harrowing escapes from death, about his liberation and his new life in America. For his every dramatic step is a lesson in God's miracles that constitute all our lives.

There is a reason that Leibel called his memoir, *I Believe*. May his belief lead all who enter into his world to discover it in themselves.

Rabbi Simon Jacobson
Gershon Jacobson Jewish Continuity Foundation
IBelieve@gjcf.com

PROLOGUE

Leibel as a boy

My father said to me, "Leibke, run!"

I was, by nature, a wild boy – a wild, red-headed kid just 13 years old. So he didn't have to tell me twice. I started to run. The Nazis could have taken their rifles and shot me, but they didn't. I guess they figured they would have a big laugh at the expense of a small Jewish child, so instead, they sent a dog after me. That German Shepherd looked as huge as a pony to me, but with God's help, I managed to outrun him for about 400 feet or so. Then he sank his teeth into the fabric of my pants. I was trying to pull away from him when, right at my feet, I saw a fallen branch; I grabbed it and zapped him on the snout as hard as I could. He let go, and I kept running. I ran around the block and then ran back to our house and hid up in the attic.

The Nazis came after me and searched the house, but I was very quiet, and they did not find me. Finally, they got tired of looking and went away.

My older brother Berel told me later that they took away my father, Shraga Feivel, along with our youngest, Chaim Yisroel, a little pipsqueak only 10 years old. They took them either to a fort outside of town and shot them with many others over an open grave, or they took them to Auschwitz to die in the gas chambers there. I do not know where my father and little brother – may their memory be forever blessed – are buried. I just know that they are dead somewhere. And I know that if my father hadn't told me to run, I would be there with them today.

But God had decreed otherwise, and I lived. And I am still alive to tell this story.

LIFE IN LITA

My name is Aryeh Leib, though I am known as Leibel – Leibel Leo Zisman. I am the son of Shraga Feivel and Leba Bluma Zisman.

I was born on Yom Kippur of the Hebrew year 5691 (תרצ"א) – that is, October 1, 1930 – in Kovno (also known as Kaunas). When I was born, Kovno was the temporary capital of independent Lithuania[4] and one of the centers of Jewish life in Lita, as we called it.

Kovno occupied a triangular piece of land between two rivers – the Nieman and the Neris – that join north of the city to flow to the Baltic Sea. On the northeast side of the triangle, across the River Neris, lay the suburb of Slobodka, the home of the famous Slobodka Yeshiva and later the site of the Kovno Ghetto. The

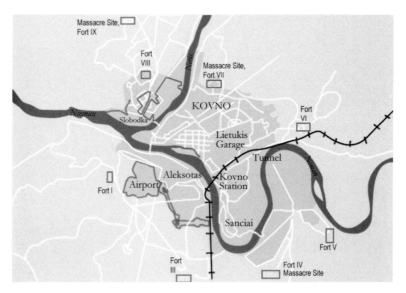

Map of Kovno

[4] Lithuania – with a Jewish population of 160,000 – was an independent state from 1918 until 1940 when it was absorbed into the USSR. On June 22, 1941 it was invaded by Germany and remained under German occupation until 1944 when it once more reverted to the USSR. With the fall of communism in 1990, it again became an independent state.

city was surrounded by nine 19th century forts, originally built as a bulwark against the enemies of the Russian Empire; these forts later became the burial sites of thousands of Jews murdered there, perhaps my beloved father and little brother included.

One of the forts outside of town, where many Jews were murdered

My family had been Chabad chassidim for five generations back, which would put my ancestors among the first followers of the Alter Rebbe,[5] the founder of the Chabad Lubavitch arm of the Chassidic Movement.

My father came from the little chassidic town of Ponedel (Pandelys) near the Latvian border. His father (Dov Ber) passed

---

[5] The Alter Rebbe, Rabbi Schneur Zalman of Liadi (1745-1812), was the founder of the Chabad arm of the Chassidic Movement. He was a student of Rabbi Dov Ber, the Maggid of Mezeritch, who in turn was a student of the Baal Shem Tov, the founder of Chassidism. The Alter Rebbe is the author of the *Shulchan Aruch HaRav* and the *Tanya*. His descendants and successors (the Chabad Rebbes) have the last name Schneersohn (or Schneerson), a form of "Schneur's son."

away when my father was a small boy, leaving a widow (Tona) and seven children. My father (born in 1898) was the youngest – he was only six years old when his father died, and he barely remembered his father, who died of a "rock," as they said then, (that is, of a tumor) in his neck. From that time his mother, my Bubbe Tona, had to cope alone.

She never remarried and, with the help of her children, she ran a general store in Ponedel located in the middle of the town near a big open marketplace. The farmers would arrive there with their horse-drawn wagons to trade all types of produce and, invariably, they would stop at her general store to buy dry goods.

My Bubbe's expertise was in mixing dyes, and I remember watching her in action when I was a young boy. The farmers came with wool from their sheep, and she would prepare a dye of whatever color they wanted. She would say, "What color do you want? Show me the color you want!" And then she would mix

Ponedel marketplace

the dyes to get the right color and soak a test batch of wool. Once the wool was dyed, the farmers' wives could spin it into yarn and knit colorful sweaters from it. My Bubbe was the one that had the magic touch and could create these beautiful colors – sky blue, viridian green, crimson red – that was her forte.

My Bubbe's store in Ponedel

Besides that, she worked in the big vegetable garden behind the store, where she also raised chickens and ducks, and she even had a little milk goat there. Each time I visited her, she'd say to me, "If you want to be healthy, you have to drink fresh milk." She would give me the milk straight from the goat while it was still warm. Now I did not want to drink this strange-tasting milk from a smelly goat, and I would refuse, but she'd bribed me with a piece of chocolate. She'd say, "Drink up. It's good for you. If you drink it all up, you'll get a piece of chocolate." So I came to look forward to those visits very much.

I knew that my Bubbe had been through a lot, though I would never have guessed it by her attitude to life. When World War I broke out in 1914 (some 16 years before I was born), she had lost her home, as the Russians who then controlled Lithuania did not trust the Jews to be so near the front lines, and banished them to Russia, to the town of Nizhniy-Novgorod on the other side of Moscow. This was really an excuse to loot and vandalize their property, but what could the poor Jews do? They were told to go, so they went. In Nizhniy-Novgorod, using what she managed to bring with her, my Bubbe set up a general store similar to the one she had in Ponedel.

During World War I, my father and his brothers were all drafted into the Russian Army. The oldest, Hirsch Leib, fled to America, and the next oldest, Yosef, managed to get an exemption because he was so near-sighted as to be nearly blind. My father never reported for duty. Whenever he needed to travel, he took along Yosef's exemption papers and his very thick glasses; when he put them on, he truly could not see, so he didn't have to make believe. One day he was traveling somewhere to buy things for Bubbe's store, and he fell asleep on the train. There was a random check of identification documents, and when the guards woke him up and looked at his eyes without the thick glasses, they refused to believe he was nearly blind, so they took him off the train. While he waited to be transported to prison for an interrogation, he got an idea. He saw a guard filling out papers by candlelight, a kettle nearby boiling water for tea. At that time, all Russians drank strong tea, which was made in a small pot called a *tcheynik*, but my father had just bought some double-sided, perforated spoons that

My father as a boy (left) with his mother Tona (my Bubbe) and his brother Yosef, who was very near-sighted

neatly held the tea leaves and allowed one to brew individual cups of tea without a *tcheynik*. So he ventured cautiously over to the guard and offered him this special spoon. The guard was so amazed by this novelty spoon and so happy to have it that he took the arrest papers, held them up to the candle and burned them. And then he told my father to disappear. My father did not have to be told twice, and he fled for home as fast as possible.

Meanwhile, my Bubbe woke up in the middle of the night with a nightmare – she had dreamt about this whole episode. She said to her daughter, my father's sister Bayla, "I dreamt that soldiers arrested Feivel, but then came Tatte [she meant her late husband, my father's father] and pushed them away. And Feivel got free!" And sure enough he came home on the next train. I heard that story many times as I was growing up because my father was very fond of telling it, always emphasizing that his own father never ceased to watch over him from beyond the grave.

When World War I ended and the Bolsheviks took over, the Jews were allowed to go home, so my Bubbe returned with her children to Ponedel and picked up where she left off, running her general store and mixing dyes. My father worked in the store, helping Bubbe make ends meet because, by then, most of his older siblings had fled Eastern Europe – his brothers went to America, two of his sisters went to South Africa and one to Israel;[6] only his youngest sister Bayla remained behind, helping her mother along with him.

My father did not want to abandon his widowed mother to go to a chassidic yeshiva in a far off place, so – although he had been educated in the chassidic way as a child under the tutelage of the holy Chabadnik Reb Yekkel Ponedeler – he enrolled in a nearby *misnagdishe* yeshiva founded by the opponents of the Chassidic

---

[6] See note I in APPENDIX for additional details.

Movement.[7] To my father, this was not an obstacle because he loved all his fellow Jews, no matter what stream of Judaism they chose to pursue, and this love showed. Besides that, he had an open and engaging personality which endeared him to anybody and everybody; thus he was not only accepted at the *misnagdishe* yeshiva but he made a mark there.[8]

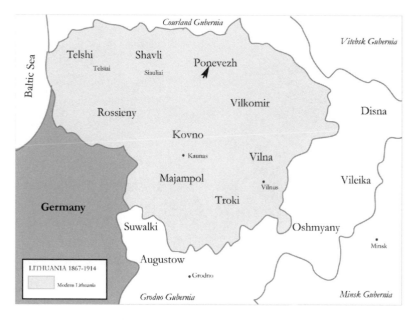

Map of Lita with Ponevezh identified

---

[7] The founding of the Chassidic Movement in the 18th century by the Baal Shem Tov (Rabbi Yisroel Ben Eliezer) – who revived the soul of Judaism – led to an initial critical reaction from some of the Jewish establishment. These opponents were called *misnagdim*.

[8] Another factor that influenced my father's choice of yeshiva was that he had an uncle – known to me only as Uncle Sheftel – living nearby. At that time the students of the yeshiva had to be fed by local families, and my father could go to Uncle Sheftel's house for his meals.

The yeshiva he chose was the famous Ponevezh Yeshiva, then under leadership of the great Rav Yosef Shlomo Kahaneman, who was known as the Ponevezher Rav. At about this time, the rabbis of Eastern Europe organized a big conference – the World Congress of Agudas Israel – in Vienna. One of the proposals at this conference was that all yeshiva students should study a page

Rav Kahaneman, my father's teacher

of the Talmud every day – what came to be called *Daf Yomi* ("Daily Page") – and that everyone, everywhere, should study the same page. This way they would all complete the entire Talmud together in seven-and-a-half years. This proposal was enthusiastically accepted and, of course, the program of daily study continues to this day, with each cycle completion accompanied by much fanfare and celebration.[9] The Ponevezher Rav was traveling to this conference and, as it was the custom for a big rabbi to travel with a student, he selected my father to accompany him, so my father was part of this great historic moment for Orthodox Jewry which took place in 1923 in Vienna.[10]

My father studied at Ponevezh until he got married in 1924. By this time his sister Bayla had also married, and she brought her husband[11] to work in my Bubbe's store, and that freed my father to spread his wings. So it happened that when he married my mother, who was the youngest daughter of Menachem Mendel Raskin and Chaya Zilpa nee Reisman[12] (a descendant of another long-standing Chabad family), he went to work for his father-in-law in Kovno.

The reason for this was practical – my Zeide had no sons who could take over the family business; his two older daughters went with their husbands, and when my father had married his youngest daughter, it fell to him to help out.

---

[9] See *New York Times*, August 1, 2012, for a report of the last such celebration, so huge it took place in MetLife Stadium, a venue large enough to accommodate its 90,000 participants.

[10] See note II in APPENDIX for additional details.

[11] See note III in APPENDIX for additional details.

[12] See note IV in APPENDIX for additional details.

The Family Business

The family business was a *gesheft* (flour store), but Zeide dealt in all kinds of wholesale commodities – not just flour, also sugar and other grains and cereals. And he resold these goods to grocers. He liked to pray and study until the middle of the afternoon while my father ran the store. With time, my father expanded the business a great deal. Besides the flour and the sugar, he began to import all kinds of non-perishable foods – beans, rice, canned goods, coffee, tea, and the like – eventually supplying his customer grocers with all the products they needed. He handled 600 different products and he had 800 customers, or maybe it was the other way around – he handled 800 different products and had 600 customers. At any rate, after the government's wholesale grocery, ours was the largest in all of Lithuania; we supplied all the little shops in the whole country – in Shavel, Memel, Telz, Kelem, Rakshik, Kupishok, Snupishok and so forth. The business – which was located in the center of Kovno, at 14 Vilna Gass – was highly respected, and life was smooth until the war broke out.

I had an older sister Tzivia (born in 1927), and an older brother Berel (born in 1929); I was the third child (born in 1930), and after me came Chaim Yisroel (born in 1934).

I was a feisty red-headed kid (called a *gingie* because of my ginger-colored hair), but I think that my brash personality served me in good stead, as proven by what happened later in the camps. Perhaps if the war had not broken out, it might have got me in trouble, but as it was, it got me through many a scrape – that and the mercy of God, Who had a plan for me.

Right to left: My father (Shraga Feivel), my older brother (Berel), me (Leibel), my mother (Leba Bluma), my sister (Tzivia), my younger brother (Chaim Yisroel). They all perished; only Berel and I survived.

Growing up in Kovno, I was a normal *yingele* born into a chassidic family. Our home was constantly filled with talk of Torah and religious matters. In some measure this was due to Zeide, who had dedicated his whole life to learning, and who came to live with us after he was widowed. At that time he was going blind and could not read the holy texts anymore, so he would recite them by heart, particularly the *Mishna*, all six orders of it. He would threaten us children with his cane if we got too loud or rambunctious because he wanted us to pay attention to every word. Unfortunately, one evening while going to the synagogue he fell down a stairway and hurt himself so badly he never came home from the hospital. I was six at the time he died.

The synagogue (*shul*) was very important to my Zeide as he had been instrumental in building it. It was a big, two-story brick building on Seyne Gass, and I so well remember going there with my father. One entered through a wide corridor into a huge room that accommodated 250 people and in the winter had to be heated by two wood stoves. All around were benches and lecterns for praying and learning, and in the middle was a raised platform (*bima*) anchored by four columns, with the holy ark (where the Torah scroll was kept) in the front. The women's section was upstairs.

Although our *shul* was mostly Chabad, it was attended by other chassidic sects as well – Gerrer chassidim, Slonimer chassidim, Kodonover chassidim and others.[13] The *shul* was not just for prayers; it was also a place for learning – it doubled as a *Beis Midrash* where young men learned Torah – and a communal hall for weddings, bar mitzvah celebrations and other festivities.

And, not the least of which, it was the site of my school, known as the *cheder*.

In Hebrew, *cheder* means "room" and that is what our school was – one side room of the synagogue. There I studied religious subjects – that is, the *Tanach*[14] and a little bit of Talmud. For secular subjects my father arranged for home-schooling by a tutor from whom my brother and I learned mathematics and a little bit

---

[13] All the chassidic sects were named after the towns in Eastern Europe where they originated. They each had a Rebbe whose dictates they followed. So it was that the Gerrer chassidim, as per their Rebbe, prayed an hour earlier than the rest, and they studied holy texts until the main group began the Torah reading, when they joined up with the others.

[14] The *Tanach* (the Hebrew Bible) is an acronym for Torah (that is, the Five Books of Moses), *Neviim* (the Prophets) and *Ketuvim* (the Writings, which include the Books of Esther, Ruth, Job, etc. as well as the Psalms and the Proverbs).

of Lithuanian (as it was required by law that everyone must be able to read and write in the native language).

What I remember about *cheder* was that there were about 25 or so kids of various ages and a teacher (called the *cheder rebbe*) whose name was Yosef Shlomo Peletz. I loved going to school. To me it was an amazing place – really *gevaldig* – even though our teacher was very strict. He let us play and be wild in the yard, but when we came in to learn, we had to behave. He had total control over the class, and when necessary he would hit us. I remember that he always wore a *sartook*, a long jacket that buttoned right over left, and he would keep his left hand tucked into this jacket Napoleon-style because he was disabled in some way; he only had partial use of that hand, but it could come snapping out of his jacket in a hurry to flatten a kid's ear.

Though he hit us sometimes, we didn't resent it because we knew that every time a *yingele* got a *potch*, he deserved it. He was very fair, and he was a wonderful teacher. He knew how to draw a picture in a child's imagination with a story. When he told a tale from the *Tanach*, I felt like I could see the whole biblical world he described. He sincerely cared about his students, and he was an excellent teacher largely because of this and because of his story-telling ability.

A Wild Child

I was a wild hyperactive kid who was always on the go. I liked playing with other kids – we played in the yard near the *cheder* and in the near-by field. We played games with buttons and with nuts, and we kicked a ball around. But even more than playing games,

I enjoyed taking things apart and putting them back together again. That was the only time I was still – when I was dismembering something. My mother used to joke that I was born with a hammer and screwdriver in my hand. I was always banging, hanging and mending. Once I disassembled and then rebuilt a bicycle; it was squeaking, and I thought I could make it run more smoothly. My father was amazed; he asked me, "How did you do that?" I said, "When I took it apart, I paid attention to how the pieces fit." This was more fun to me than playing with toys.

My daytime activities sometimes tired me out so much that I would fall asleep early and then wake up hungry in the middle of the night. I remember my mother got tired of having her sleep disrupted because I wanted something to eat, so she would put bread, butter and a glass of milk in a cupboard, and then I could help myself to a midnight snack.

So that was my childhood – it was normal, it was happy. I had a wonderful family, and I lived in a beautiful Torah environment, where Jews of all stripes got along and lived in unity. Despite the many Jewish sects represented, there was only one Kovno Rav – Rabbi Avrohom Duber Kahana-Shapiro. There was one *beis din*, the court for adjudicating disputes; there was one *shechita*, the standard for determining the kosher status of meat, and one *chevra kadisha*, the burial society. Everyone lived peacefully together. A lot is said about the historic disagreement between the chassidim and the *misnagdim*, but in Kovno before the war everyone got along like one big happy family.

This is the atmosphere in which I grew up. My childhood was particularly privileged because my father was highly respected and very successful. He was considered a *gvir* – a powerful, wealthy man – in Kovno.

Rav Kahana-Shapiro, the spiritual leader of Kovno Jewry

A big, tall man, he was very health-conscious. He would get up very early every morning and go for a long swim in the Nieman River (weather permitting). Afterwards, he would go to the *mikveh*, learn Torah and chassidic teachings (*Chassidus*), pray and then come home to eat a very large breakfast, which was the main meal of his day. After breakfast, he went to work and when he finished at the store, he would learn Torah again.[15] He did not come home till late at night, when he ate a light supper and went to bed.

In the community, my father became something of a legend. Many years later, I heard an eye-witness[16] tell a story of a *gvir* from Kovno who, in order to hear the Chabad Rebbe speak, once climbed a 30-foot column in a *shul* in Rakshik, and, in order to stay up there, tied himself to the column with his *gartel*.[17] People were crying out, "Look, look at him! The *gvir* from Kovno! The *gvir* from Kovno is hanging there!" That man was my father.

I have to say here that my father was a very dignified man – both in manner and appearance. He was a dapper dresser, always impeccably attired, his pants pressed with a crease sharp enough to cut cheese, his shoe laces covered with spats. He wore gloves and carried a cane with a silver handle. When he ate – no matter if it was a holiday feast or ordinary breakfast – he always ate slowly, formally, using a linen napkin and silver utensils, never his fingers, carefully cutting all his food into small pieces. (He'd joke that this way "it packed in better" in his stomach.) Though he was the embodiment of dignity, he did not stand on ceremony when it came to hearing the Rebbe. He would hang in the air, if that's what it took.

The Rebbe whom my father wanted so much to see and hear on that occasion in Rakshik was the Rebbe Rayatz – Rabbi Yosef Yitzchak Schneersohn – who had just been exiled from Russia

---

[15] He learned with Reb Yehoshua Yitzchak Sender, who was sent from the Chabad headquarters to be the *mashpiah* (mentor) for the Chabad chassidim in Kovno.

[16] The eye-witness was Reb Shmuel Levitin, who was the rabbi of the Rakshik synagogue. He said that the Rebbe Rayatz – that is, Rabbi Yosef Yitzchak Schneersohn (1880-1950) – spoke on the subject *Ata Echad v'Shimecha Echad* "You are One and Your Name is One."

[17] A *gartel* is a long cloth belt used by chassidim primarily during prayer.

where he had been imprisoned, tortured, and sentenced to death by the Soviets for the "crime" of teaching Torah and spreading Judaism.[18]

The Rebbe Rayatz

On another occasion, when my father got word that the Rebbe was on a train that would be crossing Lithuania, he organized a group of several hundred people (chassidim but also many others) who wanted to see the Rebbe and get a blessing from him. The group greeted the Rebbe's train just as it crossed the border into Lithuania and climbed aboard. They mostly piled into the third class wagon, though the Rebbe – who was in a wheelchair

---

[18] The Rebbe Rayatz was freed by the Soviets after a world outcry over his unjust imprisonment. Sent out of Russia via Lithuania and Latvia, he eventually settled in Otwock near Warsaw, where he re-established the Tomchei Temimim Yeshiva; he stayed there until 1939 when – after being ransomed from the Nazis – he returned briefly to Latvia, from where he immigrated to America.

– was traveling in first class. One by one, the people made their way to the Rebbe's compartment, where he graciously received each one.

After the train had made its way through the better part of the country, my father realized that the audiences were going quite slowly and that not all the people who had made the trip would have a chance to see the Rebbe before they were forced to disembark at the Latvian border. So, at the next station stop, he got off and ran to the coal-powered locomotive to speak with the train's engineer. He called down the engineer, pulled out a roll of money, and peeled off 500 *litas* (which in the currency of Lithuania amounted to a half a year's salary). He then told the man, "This is for you, and if you do what I ask you to do, I will double this sum." The engineer was more than eager to cooperate. My father said, "Blow the whistle to indicate that you are having engine trouble. Then just sit here until I come back and tell you it's time to move forward."

After a while, the Rebbe noticed that the train had been standing still for quite some time – it might have been an hour or two – and he asked his secretary to find out the source of the problem. The *gabbai* came to ask my father who said, "Please tell the Rebbe that there is a minor adjustment that has to be made to the locomotive, though how long it takes depends on the Rebbe." And when my father said this he smiled. The *gabbai* reported back to the Rebbe who immediately caught on, especially when he heard that Feivel Zisman said all this with a smile. And from then on, the audiences moved a bit faster.[19]

---

[19] This story was told to me by the *gabbai* himself, Reb Moshe Leib Rothstein, whom I later met in Brooklyn.

My father's way was always to seek a solution to the problem. This was his nature. Now, if anyone had seen my father paying off the engineer, he would have gone to prison for interfering with the workings of the railroad. But my father took the risk because he felt so badly that all these people who took off from work to greet the Rebbe would not have a chance to do so. And the Rebbe understood that and approved.

At Home

Thanks to my father's success in business, we had a very large apartment at 57 Grodno Gass, not far from the Nieman River and around the corner from my father's store. It consisted of six rooms plus a kitchen and an indoor bath (which was not so common in Lithuania then), and it was equipped with the latest in appliances available at that time. (For example, we had radiator heating, a telephone and an icebox, all of which were rare.) The apartment was so large that we had one maid to clean it and another one to do the laundry (for this purpose there was a special laundry room in the backyard and an airing room in the attic). Full-time maids were unusual in Kovno, but my mother assisted my father in the business, and she couldn't have done it without help at home.

I remember my father as big in every way – a big man with a big business and a big heart. He was so generous that, my mother used to say, if it wasn't for her, he would have given all his profits away. Of course, he contributed handsomely to all Chabad causes and to the yeshiva that the Rebbe was running in Poland.

There came a time in 1938 when the border between Poland and Lithuania opened up, so that it was possible to travel easily between the two countries, and my father made several trips to Warsaw to see the Rebbe. On the first occasion – it was the holiday of Simchas Torah – he was invited with a group of a dozen or so men to have a private meal at the Rebbe's table. He later told us how beautifully the table was set with silver and crystal (as the Rebbe's wife, the Rebbetzin Nechama Dina, was known for her aristocratic flair). They downed some vodka for *l'chaim* from crystal shot-glasses, and when they did so, my father asked the Rebbe, "May I have the vessel as well as the light?" The Rebbe smiled his consent and my father pocketed the shot-glass. When he came home, the Chabad chassidim were eager to hear all about the visit, and everyone wanted to drink out of the Rebbe's glass.

My father also raised money for poor Jews in Russia who were practicing their Judaism in secret under communist rule, acting as the Rebbe's emissary and traveling on his behalf throughout Lithuania. But more important than my father's philanthropic endeavors was the example he set as a chassid who loved all of his fellow Jews.

My father simply loved people; he was always inviting guests to our home. On Shabbos, he used to be one of the last to leave *shul*, and he would invite anyone who remained to our house – even those that perhaps were not so normal or not so clean and whom other hospitable families hesitated to invite. For him, it was the more the better, so that on a typical Shabbos we had eight to ten guests.

I remember one of the regulars was HaRav Shmuel Snieg, the Jewish chaplain in the Lithuanian army, who stopped by our house when he was on leave; I remember climbing on his lap and playing with the shiny buttons on his military uniform. Another regular guest was Eliezer Mendel, the traveling matchmaker (*shadchan*), who came into Kovno regularly to ply his trade. He always wore a very tall hat and carried a walking stick – the matchmaker's uniform.

Although my mother had maids in the house, when it came to cooking, she did not trust anyone else – not with the kosher quality of the ingredients. She herself cooked the entire Shabbos meal, which always was a grand affair – there were *forshpeiz* ("starters"), fish, soup, meat, *cholent*, fruit, dessert and, of course, something with which to say *l'chaim*.

Only once did we have no guests, and my father said to my mother that whoever was in *shul* didn't want to come. He said maybe she should change her *cholent* recipe – maybe that was the reason.

Now, my mother had her own special recipe for *cholent*, which was the centerpiece of every Shabbos meal. She made the *cholent* in a big cast-iron pot, and she knew just how much water was enough so it wouldn't burn but be well done. She would load up this pot with all the ingredients – potatoes, onions, meat bones and *kishke*, the sausage-like delicacy made from the skins of chicken necks stuffed with a paste of eggs and flour – then she'd wrap it all up in brown paper tied up with string and write our name on it with chalk. She'd send the lot to the baker (the *zetzer*), who put it in his big oven along with all the other pots that the local women sent over. He had a special way of arranging the pots so that they should not get mixed up. Coming home from *shul*, my brother Berel and I would pick up ours; I took one side and he took the other, and when we brought it back, my mother would put it in bed and cover it with a feather quilt so that it stayed hot.

As far as my brother and I were concerned, my mother's *cholent* recipe was out of this world, and we drew lots as to who got to lick out the scrapings at the bottom of the pot. We also drew lots as to who got to suck out the marrow from the bones.

I do not know if my mother altered the recipe, but very soon the guest list picked up again. As refugees started fleeing Germany and Poland, they all stayed at one time or another at our house. I remember I was always having to give up my bed to somebody; if I slept in my own bed two nights a week that was a lot. Though I had to sleep on the floor, I didn't mind because my father instilled in me that it was a big *mitzvah* to be hospitable to guests.[20]

Generous Heart

Besides being famous for having a generous heart, my father was also famous for being scrupulous in business, and he had a method of how he went about it. He would invite the salesmen – most of whom were secular Jews – into the store, give them a little schnapps, say *l'chaim* and a few words of Torah. After a half an hour, they were primed to do business.

---

[20] My father's hospitality to all Jews and his efforts, as one of the leaders of the city, on behalf of refugees are noted in *Giborei HaChayil* ("Great Heroes") by David Avraham Mandelboim.

After the war, I heard a story about my father from a salesman who survived. This incident happened when I was a baby, but it shows you why my father was a legend.

This salesman came in and offered my father a bargain – a lot of sugar had come in from Germany so there was an overstock – and the salesman told my father, "The more you buy, the lower the price will be." My father had warehouses, and he saw a good deal, so he agreed to buy the lot. He drew up a contract according to the agreed-upon formula – the greater the quantity, the lower the price per sack. And the salesman went away happy.

Two days later, though, he returned, shamefaced. "I can't deliver the sugar," he said. "The way we calculated the formula, I ended up giving you a deal below the rock-bottom cost. If I were to give you the whole lot at this price, I'd have to pay the difference out of my own pocket, and I'd be bankrupt."

My father asked to see the original contract, and he also pulled out his own copy – in those days they were written with blue carbon copies – and he studied the papers for a moment. Then he said, "I am in the business to make money, but I am not going to make money at the expense of another Jew." And with that he ripped up both copies of the contract into little pieces.

The salesman could not believe it. He started to cry, and he hugged and kissed my father. He was so happy, and the story became the talk of the town. That is why my father was a legend – his honesty and his integrity preceded him wherever he went. He could be a tough negotiator, but he always put his Torah values above making money. This I heard from many people who knew him.

He was treated with great respect wherever he went, and this was because he treated others with respect. King Solomon says in the Book of Proverbs, "As a face answers to a face in water, so does one man's heart to another,"[21] meaning that the relationship each person has with another is like a face that is mirrored in water – when one is smiling, the reflection also will be smiling; when one is scowling, the reflection will be scowling as well; for just like water, each heart mirrors the other. This is what my father knew, and this is how my father lived. And this is how he brought out the best in the people he encountered, whether they were his fellow Jews (no matter what their religious bent) or non-Jews, the *goyim* as we called them.

Despite his success and stature in town, my father always acted like a plain, ordinary person – he was always warm and kind, and best of all, he was the most loving father a kid could have. He had a *gevaldike* ability to learn with high-minded people and, a half-hour later, to go sledding with his kids. There was a hill near the river, and I so well remember flying down that snowy hill with him, his long beard blowing in the wind. As dignified as he could be with his business associates, he could be just as child-like and playful with his children. We never feared him; we loved him unconditionally, and we treasured the time we got to spend with him. Our greatest joy was listening to his stories – he was a wonderful story-teller, and he held us spellbound. And though we were wild sometimes, he never punished us.

Only once in my life did he spank me. On this occasion, I got it into the *gingie* head of mine to break all the windows on Vilna Gass. This was a street of shops, and all the shops had small

---

[21] Proverbs 27:19.

basement windows at the level of my shoe. I kicked one, and it broke; the tinkling glass made a nice sound. So I proceeded like this right on down the street. Naturally, there was an uproar, and my father was informed that a red-headed boy (there was only one who fit that description) had broken all the windows. I well remember how angry he was – which was a rare sight. I knew by then that my father was a good and patient man, but you better not cross him – he was fierce when he was angry. On this occasion he said to me, "I am not going to punish you now, because I am too angry, and the Torah teaches that we should never rebuke anyone in anger. But I want you to know that you should never in your life hurt another person or that person's property. Never!" That was it. Two days later, he called me in again, and he said, "Now I am no longer angry at you, so I will punish you. I love you and I don't want to punish you, but you must be punished for what you did." And then he spanked me.

That was my Tatte.

Tatte and Mamme

Tatte's best friend was Mamme. Rather than objecting to the stream of guests he constantly brought into the house – to feed and, in one case, to nurse to health over an extended period – she not only rose to the occasion each time, but she encouraged him. Moreover, she was his sounding board in all matters. Whenever he needed advice, he would ask her, "What do you think? Should I buy? Not buy?" And she would answer, "I have to think it over." I got the impression that while my father was great with people, my mother was better with numbers. They made a winning team working in the store together. Also working there was my Cousin Sima,[22] who was quite brilliant in her own right and could write simultaneously with both hands (though not on different topics). But I knew her more by reputation then, because when I was a toddler she left for America to get married.

Sima was the oldest daughter of my mother's sister, my Aunt Tzivia,[23] who had 13 children, all of them equally brilliant. One, named Gershon, could recite the alphabet when he was still nursing at his mother's breast; another, Dvosha, age five, knew the whole Book of Psalms by heart; and the teenager, Leibel, was such a holy boy that, when beaten by the Nazis, he would only say that he accepted his suffering with love. They were very unusual children of a very unusual woman – Aunt Tzivia, who was recognized to be both learned and holy. She taught women's classes in Kabbalah, and sometimes wrote letters asking questions of the Rebbe Rayatz. Now, anyone could write the Rebbe and get an answer, but Aunt Tzivia got five-page letters back, which meant her questions were quite scholarly and complex. However, she never displayed her knowledge in front of men, not wanting to embarrass her husband. I once heard my mother say that Aunt Tzivia secretly wore *tzitzis*[24] under her dress. It was unheard of for women to wear this (though it is not forbidden by Jewish law). My mother used to laugh about it and say *mein frumme shvester* ("my pious sister").

Besides being busy in the store, my mother was very involved in various projects in the community. She always organized a

---

[22] See note VII in APPENDIX for additional details.

[23] See note VIII in APPENDIX for additional details.

[24] *Tzitzis* is a short-hand reference to the *tallis katan* – a small four-cornered garment with specially knotted fringes called *tzitzis* that men are required by the Torah to wear, so that they remember its commandments.

My Tatte and Mamme

special celebration for *Yud-Tes Kislev*.[25] She would make *klops* which was a special meat-loaf with a hard-boiled egg inside, and my father would get a barrel of beer and also vodka for *l'chaim*. Other families that could afford it would prepare food as well. The feast was held in the *shul*, and it was always a very happy occasion.

---

[25] This was a celebration of the Alter Rebbe's rescue. In 1778, he was accused of treason and imprisoned by the Russian czar for sending money to Jews in the Land of Israel (then in the hands of Russia's enemy, the Ottoman Empire); but on *Yud-Tes* (19th day of) *Kislev* he was set free. Ever since, the date has been joyfully marked by Chabad chassidim, as a day that vindicated the Alter Rebbe and his spreading of *Chassidus*.

My parents also often helped poor families make a wedding. They would hire a one-man band, and my mother would organize the community women to prepare the food – such were the customs of the Jews in Kovno. Also, from time to time, my Uncle Pinchas (Aunt Tzivia's husband), who was a *mohel* trained to do circumcisions, would tell my father about a poor family who could not afford the requisite celebratory meal, and then my father and my mother would take care of everything.

Kovno was a city of about 150,000 people, 35,000 of them Jews.[26] The Kovno Jews were not particularly religious, and there were quite a few *maskilim* (the so-called "enlightened"). There

My Aunt Tzivia

[26] In 1940, the census showed an estimated 154,000 total people in Kovno, one-quarter of them Jews. The city had almost one-hundred Jewish organizations, forty synagogues, Yiddish schools, four Jewish newspapers, four Hebrew high schools, a Jewish hospital, and scores of Jewish-owned businesses.

were lawyers and doctors. The religious people were of the Ashkenazi persuasion – what you would call *Litvak Yeshivish* today – and they had close to 50 synagogues. The chassidim were a minority – I would estimate there were only about 500 chassidic families in Kovno and its suburbs. They belonged to various chassidic sects, with Chabad being dominant, not only in numbers but in community activities as well. Each family was eager to participate in works of kindness, and my father was always at the forefront – organizing, contributing, helping bring Jews of different stripes together.

That was the picture of Jewish life in Kovno until the war broke out. Until then, the anti-Semitism was not in the open, and the Lithuanians behaved well toward the Jews. This was because the president at the time, Antanas Smetona[27] suppressed any anti-Semitic activity; he was a democrat, and he hated communism. The religious Jews voted for him, and he gave the rabbis a place of honor when it came to Lithuanian national celebrations. His wife made a point of buying in Jewish stores, and when she was asked why, she said, "They treat me better." So this president, while he lasted, kept anti-Semitism down, but all that changed, of course.

Hitler marched into Poland in September of 1939. I still remember hearing the news and seeing my father shaking with emotion. He must have sensed that terrible things were about to come.

But, immediately, there was one positive result. The Rebbe Rayatz, who had been living in Otwock near Warsaw at the time

---

[27] Antonas Smetona fled to the United States when Stalin invaded Lithuania; an anti-communist, he died in a fire in Cleveland in 1944 which many believe was intentionally set.

when Hitler started bombing the city, was ransomed out and, after many travails, was permitted to leave for Latvia, as he had Latvian citizenship.[28] The Rebbe stayed in Riga for a few months before going to America and, at the beginning of March 1940, my father took me to see him. (My brother had been taken to get a blessing from the Rebbe when he was still in Poland, so now it was my turn.)

Blessing from the Rebbe

It was a very special occasion to meet the Rebbe and to get a blessing from him. Chabad chassidim believe that the Rebbe carries a spark of *Moshe Rabbeinu* (Moses, our Teacher, our first Rebbe) and is a very high soul with special spiritual strengths and abilities to intercede on our behalf with God. I saw proof of this with the blessing he gave my Aunt Bayla from Ponedel. After being married for ten years, Aunt Bayla and Uncle Yankel had had no children, and every doctor they went to told them it was impossible. But when they asked the Rebbe Rayatz to give them a blessing to have a child, Aunt Bayla immediately got pregnant. I was six years old when she gave birth, which was a sensation, and I remember the fanfare at the *bris* of this miracle child.

When we arrived at the Rebbe's home in Riga, we first went in to visit the Rebbetzin Shterna Sarah, the Rebbe's mother, who was recovering from an operation. Thus we fulfilled the *mitzvah* of visiting the sick. My father was thrilled that the Rebbetzin took an interest in me and gave me a *sukarke*, a hard candy in a colorful wrapper. Outside, hundreds of people were milling about waiting

---

[28] The story of his escape is documented in *Out of the Inferno* by Rachel Altein.

to see the Rebbe, so we had a very long wait – it wasn't till 2 or 3 in the morning that our turn came. While we were waiting, my father picked me up and stood me on top of a cabinet near the door, so that whenever someone went in or out, I could get a peek at the Rebbe. Finally, we were admitted. I remember my father walked in, approached the Rebbe (who was seated behind a desk), greeted him and then took a few steps back. My father told me that one never sat in front of the Rebbe, but it was also rude to hover over him, so out of respect one took a few steps back. My father and the Rebbe conversed for a few minutes, and then my father asked the Rebbe to bless me.

At this moment, the Rebbe looked at me. He had a powerful stare, his eyes boring into the person as if seeing the core of one's soul. I felt his eyes going through me, and I was scared. I heard my father ask the Rebbe again to please bless me, but the Rebbe just continued to stare. It was as if he was looking through me into some abyss. I started to tremble. And then I heard my father's voice cracking with emotion, "Rebbe, please, please bless my boy! *Rebbe, Rebbe! Bentsch mein yingele! Bentsch mein yingele!*" And he began to cry.

It seemed like time stopped still – my father sobbing, me shaking and the Rebbe staring with his x-ray eyes – but then, finally, the Rebbe pronounced the blessing.

But why did he hesitate? What did he see? What forces were arrayed against me? Was it my father's broken plea that finally swayed him? And is this why I and my brother, who also got a blessing a few years prior, survived when everyone else in our family perished?

I will be asking those questions to my dying day.

The Rebbe left Riga that night (March 4, 1940). People were begging him to stay because so many were waiting to see him and be blessed by him; people were particularly desperate at this time because the war had started, Czechoslovakia and Poland had been seized by Germany, and the air was thick with evil portents. But the Rebbe would not delay. He told his secretary that his father – the Rebbe Rashab who had passed away some 20 years before – would not allow him to stay. He did not explain if his father came to him in a vision or in a dream, but he insisted on leaving immediately with his whole family despite his mother's poor medical condition.

My father organized a human shield to keep back the crowd, as the ambulance pulled up to the building to take away the Rebbetzin on a stretcher. Everyone was crying, fearful they would never see the Rebbe again, and it was a very chaotic scene. As it happened, the Rebbe boarded the last plane leaving Riga for Stockholm, and from there, he boarded the last boat for America. After that, it was near impossible for anyone to get out. By June of 1940, Stalin (Hitler's ally at the time) took over Latvia and Lithuania.

Russian Invasion

When the Russians came in – tanks rolling through town – the Lithuanian government fled to Germany. Now communist rule prevailed. Immediately all large businesses were nationalized because, under the communist system, private enterprise was not permitted. Small concerns – the shoemaker, the tailor, the grocer – were permitted to carry on, but my father's business was too big, and he lost his store. Anyone who was not a common laborer was called a bourgeoisie, which was the same as being a criminal. A lot of the bourgeoisie, such as factory owners, big businessmen, doctors, lawyers, intellectuals, were deported to Siberia, but my father had friends in high places, and they warned him when the police were coming to pick him up. We made sure not to be home – we all went to stay with relatives in the country for awhile – and eventually they gave up. Little by little, life returned to normal, if you could call it that.

Under communism, religious studies were forbidden. Since an essential part of Judaism is the constant learning of Torah, just being a religious Jew meant one was breaking the law. Despite this, Jewish education continued. Although the Slobodka Yeshiva was closed down, the students found an extra room in a nearby synagogue to continue their studies. Of course, the youth were

Map of Lithuania, Latvia and Poland in 1939-40

encouraged to join clubs where communist ideology was taught, and those who learned well were awarded a shining red star. Unfortunately, secular Jews joined hands with the Soviets; they were the ones who believed that "from each according to his ability, to each according to his need." So it was that these Jews became commissars, trying to indoctrinate communist ideas in others[29] and oppressing their own people as well as the Lithuanians.

At first, the commissars in Kovno who took over my father's store let him stay on as a "manager," but after three months, after they had learned the business, they fired him. Being unemployed was an even worse offense than being a bourgeoisie, so my father quickly got another job – as a watchman. That, too, lasted a very short time because the Soviets had a six-day week – everybody rotated working five days with the sixth day off. When my father's turn came around to work on Shabbos, naturally he could not, so that was the end of that.

To make money, my father started dealing in gold and hard currency. A lot of refugees were coming through, many of them – most of them, it seemed like to me – staying with us, and they brought things with them which they wanted to sell. At the same time, whoever could was trying to get out of Eastern Europe, and they wanted to buy. So my father had a brisk business going.

Kovno was such a draw for refugees because the US, Dutch and Japanese consulates were located there. Now, the Americans had quotas and lists and application forms, and the Dutch likewise allowed only a limited number of Jews to immigrate to their colonies, but the hero of the moment proved to be the Japanese

[29] See note IX in APPENDIX for additional details.

consul, Chiune Sugihara,[30] who made it his mission to save Jewish lives. Disregarding his own superiors' instructions, he hand-wrote visas, sending thousands of Jews to Shanghai which had a large Jewish community and which was then in Japanese hands. This is how he saved the whole Mir Yeshiva and the Lubavitch Tomchei Temimim Yeshiva as well. On his last night in Kovno, he stayed up all night writing visas, and even as he boarded the train he was still writing – knowing that every slip of paper saved a life – and throwing them out the window to the begging throngs. I did not see this, but I heard the story told with much emotion by survivors.[31]

By then word was out that the Zisman house welcomed all refugees and lots more came. Believe me, lots more came. To camouflage all these people coming and going, my father opened a small restaurant in our home, since such an establishment, though private, was insignificant enough as to be permitted under communist law. During the day, 20 to 30 people came in to have a meal (the refugees ate for free) and to do business "under the table." My mother did most of the cooking with a helper. If anyone we didn't know came in, we just pretended it was a restaurant, served them a meal and kept all other activity out of sight.

I do not know why my father didn't decide right then and there to pack up and go to America. I don't know. He had older brothers, so we could have had sponsors. It could have happened. Even when the Rebbe himself went to Brooklyn in March of

---

[30] The Simon Wiesenthal Center has estimated that Chiune Sugihara issued transit visas for about 6,000 Jews and that about 40,000 descendants of the Jewish refugees are alive today because of him. In 1985, Israel honored him with its "Righteous Among the Nations" award for his heroic actions.

[31] See note X in APPENDIX for additional details.

1940, there was opportunity. But, by the time my father decided we needed to go, he could not get us visas. The various foreign consulates had moved out to Moscow – as Lithuania had ceased to exist and was now part of the USSR – and he could not get permission to travel there. And once the Nazis came (in June 1941) any remaining slim chance was gone.

Had my father suspected how grave the danger really was, he would have paid whatever it cost to get us smuggled into Moscow, or to get us visas – even if not to America, then to Stockholm or Shanghai. My father certainly had the money.

What can I tell you? This was *bashert* – this had to be.

KOVNO GHETTO

On a sunny Sunday in June – June 22, 1941 to be precise – Hitler invaded the USSR and that meant he also invaded Lithuania. When this happened I was only ten, and my memory of that day is poor. I do remember the chaos that ensued with the Russians retreating, sirens going off, and transportation and communication disrupted – you could not call anybody and you could not go anywhere.

That night, there was a meeting in our house of a group of chassidim, to decide what to do: run deep into Russia or stay and face the Germans? They reached the decision to stay put, as they did not know then what the Germans were planning. They had heard some news of German atrocities in Poland – like the burning of synagogues filled with people – but they could not fathom that Hitler planned a total annihilation of the Jews. Further, they reasoned that chances of a successful escape were slim, and they expected no better treatment at the hands of Russian communists, who had a history of abusing religious Jews and particularly Lubavitch chassidim.

Some people did run, and most of them did not make it. They were killed – not by the Germans, who had not yet reached Kovno, but by the Lithuanians. At this time there was a terrible Lithuanian backlash against the communists, and it gave vent to their innate anti-Semitism as well. During the time that Lithuania was independent, anti-Semitism was suppressed; Jews, as citizens, had equal rights. Then, during the Soviet domination, some secular Jews even achieved power, serving as commissars in the communist regime. Now, the Lithuanians joined hands with the Nazis, and woe to any Jew who crossed their path. They did not care that religious Jews had not collaborated with the Soviets; they just went out on a killing spree.

We locked our doors and shuttered our windows. Fortunately, because of the restaurant business, we had extra food, so we could stay in the house until their rage was spent, but pity those who had to go out on the street or lived in vulnerable houses.

Round-up of Jews by the Lithuanians

Aftermath of massacre of Jews carried out by the Lithuanians

There was a massacre in Slobodka. My brother remembers that when my father was looking for a place for us because we had to move into the ghetto which was to be in Slobodka, he walked into an empty house and saw an unimaginable sight – blood everywhere, bloodied walls, beds soaked in blood, even a bloody crib where a little baby had once slept.

The Lithuanians had murdered 700 Jews in Slobodka on one night of rampage alone – and they had just begun. Before they were through, 6,000 Kovno Jews were dead.

Then the Nazis came into the city, embraced and cheered by the Lithuanians, and the decrees started – all aimed at the Jews. No Jew could be seen on the street between certain hours; no Jew could stroll in the park or sit on a park bench; every Jew had to wear a Star of David on the front and back; and every Jew had a month to move to a specially designated area of town.

At this time, we had a terrible scare. A morning *minyan*[32] had gathered in our home and the men were praying, all of them wearing their *tefillin* and *talleisim*, when suddenly, there was a knock on the door. A high-ranking German officer, judging by his decorations, marched in, followed by two soldiers armed with rifles. He looked around and then ordered everyone to go out to the backyard. The men were terrified, fully expecting to be shot, especially when they were ordered to line-up against the wall. But, instead, the Germans took out cameras and started taking pictures, and then they said everybody could go back inside. What did that mean? Were they just playing with us, terrorizing us with cameras? Were they innocently curious, fascinated by Jewish

[32] A group of ten men required for formal prayers.

customs which they found strange? Or, were they documenting the lives of the Jews of Kovno since they planned to annihilate them all bit by bit? As it turned out, it was the latter.

Of the 35,000 Jews then living in the greater Kovno area, 20% of the poorest lived in Slobodka, a run-down suburb of old wooden houses with few accoutrements. Now *all* Jews were ordered to squeeze into Slobodka, which would become known as the "Kovno Ghetto." We had until August 15, 1941. By then, every Jew had to be in the ghetto. Every Jew.

Of course, there were also non-Jews living in Slobodka at this time, but they were forced to leave. My father, who spoke perfect Lithuanian, struck a deal with a local who owned a large wooden house in Slobodka. It was divided into four two-room apartments, and it had a spacious attic, a small root cellar and a big garden. It was quite primitive compared to what we were used to – it had no indoor plumbing; there was just a well in a yard and a three-compartment outhouse, each compartment consisting of a wooden seat with a hole in the middle positioned over a cesspool in the ground. Try sitting on that in the middle of the winter. Still, this was the best of a bad lot, and my father made a trade with the owner – in exchange for his place, my father gave him a brick apartment house of 16 units with indoor plumbing located in the Kovno suburb known as Grine Barg ("Green Hill"). It was hardly a fair deal, but what could we do – at least we got a half-decent place to live. Many other people had it a lot worse.

Later, my brother would say that the location of the house was ideal. It was off the major streets and not near the fences or gates where we would be more conspicuous. When inches and minutes made a difference as to who would be taken to die and who would be left behind to live a few more days, such things mattered very much.

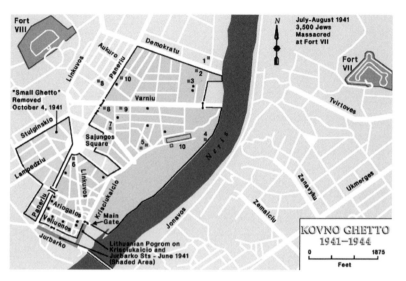

Map of Kovno Ghetto

Street inside Kovno Ghetto

Wagons moving Jews into the ghetto

And so we went there – with *pecklach*, with bundles. My father hired someone with a horse and wagon, and we took what we could – pots and pans, pillows, blankets, clothes, books. My father smuggled in a Torah scroll, and he also packed a suitcase full of grain, thinking ahead to next Passover when he would have to make *matzos*, for he valued his Torah obligations more highly than any of his possessions. In fact, most of them – all the furniture and the big expensive items – we were forced to leave behind in Kovno. And we never saw them or our home again.

Behind Barbed Wire

They surrounded the whole ghetto[33] with barbed wire, and they locked us in. There were only a few well-guarded gates out of the place, manned by vicious Lithuanian guards. I never saw them though. For three years I did not leave the ghetto. The only time I left the ghetto was the day they put me on the train bound for the death camps.

One of the gates into Kovno ghetto

Wooden bridge connecting parts of the ghetto

[33] The ghetto actually had two parts, as Slobodka was divided in half by a large thoroughfare. Over this, a wooden footbridge was built to connect the larger section (near the Neris River) with the smaller one (on the east side of town). After a series of selections, the ghetto population dwindled, and the small ghetto was closed, with any remaining people herded into the west side of town.

As we were moving into the ghetto, a Jewish Committee was organized to prevent chaos. The Germans insisted on this. The committee had to make sure the Jews moved to this "gated community" in Slobodka in an orderly way. And we did. We went in like sheep. What else could we do? Yes, there were a few Jewish partisans who, instead of going to the ghetto, escaped into the forest. Apparently we used to get some signals from them, but I was too young to really know about it.

I did overhear things from time to time as HaRav Snieg, the former chaplain who was a good friend of my father, was a member of the Jewish Committee, and he would bring us news. After the rampage of the Lithuanians, the Germans told the committee that the ghetto was for our own good as it would serve "to protect the Jews against such lawless acts." This was an example of the lies they routinely told with a smile on their lips.

They had some sense of humor. Fun for them was beating up a Jew. My cousin, also named Leibel, was beat up so brutally by the Gestapo that he was bruised from head to toe. My mother and my aunt covered him with cold compresses and only his youth kept him alive; an older person would not have survived a beating like that.

We occupied only one of the four apartments in our ghetto house; with so many people unable to find a roof over their heads, it would have been unconscionable to take up more than the bare minimum space required. Other families moved in with us – thankfully, Uncle Pinchas and Aunt Tzivia and all their children were among them; it was easier living with relatives. Our apartment consisted of two rooms – in one room we slept, in the other we cooked and ate. Our family at this time was just five –

my parents, my two brothers and me, because it so happened that when the war broke out, my sister Tzivia was visiting Bubbe in Ponedel, and that was the last time we heard from her.

What happened to Tzivia? What happened to Bubbe? My parents didn't talk about it. I am sure that they hoped and prayed for the best and feared the worst, but they had no way of finding anything out as all mail service had stopped; all telephones and telegraphs were cut. We could not communicate with anyone outside the ghetto. Our chief concern each day was how to make it to the next day.

My father got a job as a manager of the food distribution in the ghetto. He was chosen for this job by the Jewish Committee because he was known as an honorable, trustworthy man, who knew how to manage such a big enterprise, which involved organizing the distribution of the available foodstuffs according to the permitted rations.

My father's job was a big blessing because that meant he did not have to go out of the ghetto to work on one of the dirty jobs – like the Flugplatz ("Airfield") – that many of the men were conscripted to do. Over there they had to clear the ground of rocks with hoes, and it was back-breaking work. But even they did not complain much, because anyone who worked was useful, and anyone who was useful lived.

There came a time, about five or six weeks after the ghetto was established, when the Germans decided they only needed 5,000 workers, and they ordered the Jewish Committee to issue only that many work cards. Fearing that everyone else would be deemed dispensable, the committee refused. Anyone who knew this lived in terrible fear of what would happen next.

I did not know. I was just a little kid back then. I did not see when they took the Jews from the "small ghetto" – that is, from the area across the big road that divided Slobodka – and marched them to one of the military forts on the outskirts of town, where they murdered them all.

Grois Aktzia

Then, a few weeks later – on October 28, 1941 – the *Grois Aktzia* took place in the Demokratu Square, an open piece of land at the edge of the ghetto. I remember that the weather was turning cold and it was raining, but despite that, everybody was ordered to leave their homes at the crack of dawn, when it was still dark, and stand in the rain to be counted. Everyone, without exception, had to come or be shot on the spot, and all did – families clinging together, everyone afraid of what was to be. I remember the cold – it was so very cold – and I remember shivering as we stood there in the rain seemingly forever.

My brother remembers more. He remembers that we stood for three hours before the *selektzia* started. Then the Gestapo men and the SS, dressed in their uniforms and shining boots, got up on the raised mound that overlooked the mass of gathered people. We had to march in front of them, prodded by the Lithuanian guards, as the German officer in charge shouted, "You go here. You go there." At first, people did not understand what was happening. Sometimes when a family was being broken up, a person would cry and plead, "Oh, please, can I go there with them?" Then they would laugh. "You'd rather go there? Go there!" They knew that the poor soul just asked to go to die.

The records show that the *selektzia* took twelve hours. And, when it was over, 10,000 people – about a third of the ghetto population by that time – had been marked for death, while a crowd of Lithuanian spectators watched from a distance with delight. Twelve hours we stood in the cold, trembling in fear, until they said that those on the good side could go home. The people on the wrong side were marched to one of the forts – the Ninth Fort – outside of town.[34]

For the next two days we heard the incessant bursts of machine gun fire as they systematically murdered them all. A woman who managed to survive under a pile of corpses crawled out and came back to the ghetto to tell of what had happened. But I only learned about that later, just as I learned that, in the Ninth Fort alone, some 45,000 Lithuanian Jews were buried in 15 mass graves. Later, the Nazis had these pits dug up and the remains burned. It took months to accomplish this deed, and the air over the ghetto was filled with the acrid smoke of the burning corpses. Long before I arrived at Auschwitz, I knew what a burning human being smelled like.

On the day of the *Grois Aktzia*, we lost a lot of relatives to the Ninth Fort. Aunt Tzivia, my mother's brilliant sister, and her husband Uncle Pinchas and many of their 13 children were taken then.[35] But three were somehow spared, and they came to live with us in our part of the apartment. There were Chana and Osna (who were teenagers) and Dvosha, (who was five). My mother

---

[34] Shalom Eilati, a boy of about my age, witnessed this march and described it in his memoir, *Crossing the River.*

[35] As I said, the eldest, Sima, went to America in 1933, and another daughter, Nechama, married a Dutch citizen, Nathan Gutwirth, and was able to immigrate with him to Indonesia (Dutch East Indies) in 1940. They were the only two of my Aunt Tzivia's 13 children who survived the Holocaust.

made a curtain and divided the kitchen in two, so they had a place to sleep; we five slept in the other room.

Chana and Osna went to work and later were taken from their jobs in another *aktzia*, and we never saw them again. Dvosha stayed longer until she too perished in one of the *aktzias*, but I don't remember which one.[36] I do remember that she limped and that she used to recite the Book of Psalms like a grown-up. Though she was small, she knew how to pronounce all the words in Hebrew, and my father would give her a cookie and tell her, "Go ahead, you say *Tehillim*." And she did.

My father used to get up early himself to recite *Tehillim*. And then he went to pray with a *minyan*. At first this was possible, but later the synagogues were closed (though we organized a *minyan* in our house for Shabbos) and all holy books confiscated (though we hid some in our attic, including our Torah scroll).[37] They were trying to wipe out anything that had to do with Judaism, right down to forbidding Jews to have beards.

But my father refused to cut off his beard, and one day when he was in the food distribution center, a German officer came in and started slashing at it with a knife. He chopped off half before he was interrupted by something. My father left it like that. He took a scarf and wrapped it around his face. This is what people used to do when they had a toothache, and that is how he went around until it grew back in. He was the only Jew, besides HaRav Shapiro, who had a beard.

---

[36] I found out later that Chana and Osna were taken to the Kloga Work Camp in Estonia, where they died among 20,000 others. Dvosha was but one of the 136,421 Jews of Lita murdered by February 1942, according to the meticulously-kept German records. See *Hidden History of the Kovno Ghetto*, published by the US Holocaust Memorial Museum.

[37] The *aktzia* against books took place on February 18, 1942. On that day, Jews were forced to surrender all their books, and while some 100,000 books were confiscated then, many people risked their lives to save sacred texts from destruction.

My father simply refused to compromise any part of his Torah observance. There came a time when the Jewish Committee could not meet the quota of laborers that the Nazis demanded for a work detail, and they told my father he had to fill in. This was in the winter, and he had to leave the house early in the morning when it wasn't light yet, coming back when it was dark already. His problem then became when to put on *tefillin*, since Jewish law says it has to be worn during day hours. He decided to put on the *tefillin* before he left, go to work like that and wear it all day. It was easy to conceal the arm *tefillin* under his coat and gloves, but hiding the head *tefillin* was hard, so he wore a large felt hat on his head. And he got away with it.

Farming in the Ghetto

In the spring, my father – ever adaptable to any situation that life presented him – became a farmer. His foray into agriculture started by accident. Like everybody, we had a compost heap in the back of the house, where we dumped our garbage and, in the spring, this compost heap started to sprout tomato seedlings. My father, my brother Berel and I went to work – hoeing our garden plot and planting more seedlings – and, before long, we had a whole tomato crop – 150 kilos. In fact, we had an overabundance of tomatoes, and since tomatoes have a short shelf-life, we used them as barter. We traded them for things we needed like sugar and butter.

Then my father noticed that our next door neighbors, who were elderly people, had an even larger garden, but they did nothing with it, so my father asked if he could farm their plot as well. They said, "We're too tired to do anything with it. If you want it,

A garden in the ghetto

it's yours." So we planted potatoes there and were surprised at how well they grew – we had bags and bags of potatoes. We gave some to the neighbors whose land it was, and we traded some for other things we needed.

That's how my father got winter boots for my brothers and me. Except he didn't have much choice about sizes and mine were much too big at the top. My feet fit well with three pairs of socks, but the tops were so wide I could stuff my long johns and my pants inside with room left over; that's how big they were. This proved to be a good thing, because when I was taken from the ghetto, I was able to hide all kinds of things in those boots, especially that most precious object which I needed to pray properly – my *tefillin*. But that was much later.

For Passover, my father made sure we had *matzos*. As I said, when we moved to the ghetto my father hid away a suitcase full of wheat. Even when there was not much food, he refused to let us touch that wheat. Come *Pesach*, he found two smooth stones, and he ground that wheat into flour with which to bake *matzos*. We had a brick wood-burning oven in the kitchen and underneath it, level with the floor, there was a narrow opening where it was possible to bake two *matzos* at a time. I lay on my belly putting the *matzos* in there to bake, and when they were done, my father wrapped them in a clean *shmattah* and hung them from the ceiling in the kitchen. He did this for two reasons – so that the mice wouldn't get to them, and so that no one would see.

The next year, my father bartered tomatoes for flour and over time accumulated enough to make *matzos* again. He was so careful with this flour, he sifted it and kept it dry so that we could properly observe Passover.

My father also made wine for the *Seder*. This process he had perfected in the years before the war, largely because in Lithuania we didn't have any grapes, as this kind of semi-tropical fruit could not be grown in such a cold climate. But we could buy raisins. My father would put the raisins in a clean container, add some water and sugar and let this mixture ferment. It took months; he would start at Chanukah to have it ready by Passover. Then he would strain the resulting liquid through a clean linen handkerchief. He had to do this several times – at first the strained liquid was a muddy brown color but after he strained it several times, it became clearer. He would put it in a glass and hold it up to the sunlight, checking the clarity. (He must have had a secret formula – how much sugar, how many raisins, how much water – because as many times as I have tried, I have yet to replicate his results.) When he was satisfied that it was ready, he bottled it and sealed the cork with wax. Then it was ready and waiting.

These things my father always did at night – partly so the Germans wouldn't come and catch us, and partly so the neighbors should not see. After so much deprivation and terror, the camaraderie that we knew in Kovno before the war had worn down. You did not know whom to trust. Could your neighbor, for a loaf of bread, inform on you? So it was better that the neighbors didn't know. We were friendly with our neighbors, but we were also careful.

Of course, my father had a reputation – he had been a legend in Kovno. He had been known as an honest *gvir* before we went into the ghetto, and if anything, his reputation as an upstanding Jew only increased inside. People used to come by to get inspiration from him. My brother Berel once opened the door to a man who did not live in our part of the ghetto; it was late and this man was exhausted after a long day of work. When he came in, my father asked him, "What are you doing here?" And the man said, "I pass by here with the hope that maybe I'll find you in, and so I'll be a little inspired with some words of Torah on my way out."[38]

Being so firmly committed to Torah, my father believed that it was important that my brothers and I continue the *limudei kodesh* we had started in *cheder*, despite the fact that being caught in the act meant an instant death sentence. A few others agreed with my father. Rabbi Ephraim Oshry,[39] the assistant to the Kovno

---

[38] See note XI in APPENDIX for additional details.

[39] After the war, Rabbi Ephraim Oshry wrote a book entitled *She'alot U'teshuvot Mima'amakim* ("Out of the Depths: Questions and Answers") which was published in English as *Responsa from the Holocaust.* In this book he related the questions that Jews of Kovno asked of their Rav during this trying time, such as: "Who should receive a worker's permit, a ticket to life?" Or: "Is is permissible for an underage boy to put on *tefillin* in case he won't live to celebrate his Bar Mitzvah?" Or: "Is it permissible to give Jewish children to non-Jews, knowing they might be led to abandon their religion?"

Rav, Rabbi Avrohom Duber Kahana-Shapiro, organized a weekly Torah study program called *Tiferet Bachurim*. It was more like a club than a school, where we – 40 or 50 boys – gathered together to sing songs, hear stories from the Talmud, learn the Torah portion of the week, and to be reminded that God runs the world, that He is in charge, even in this place.

That is what we learned on Shabbos, because during the week even we, little children, had to work. My brother and I worked in the bakery for a time, where we got to lick pots as payment for our labors, so we didn't mind. Generally, it was believed that if you worked, you had a better chance of not being taken from the ghetto, so everybody did something. Nobody had to be forced to work; the Germans had a ready and willing supply of slave labor.

Rabbi Ephraim Oshry, who led the *Tiferet Bachurim* ("Beautiful Boys")

Slave Labor

The men and some of the women did various work for the Germans in factories and warehouses. Some did sewing and knitting. Some prepared shoes and boots, because the German army going into Russia had to have heavier gear. Some worked in the kitchens that supplied the soldiers. They peeled potatoes and brought home the peels to make potato-peel pies and cakes. On the road to and from the ghetto (to jobs like the Flugplatz), it was possible to barter with the Lithuanians – to trade jewelry or clothes for food. This was illegal, of course, and punishment was death, but people took risks in order to feed their families.

In the ghetto itself, there were workshops – especially created by the Jewish Committee – to employ those who were not strong enough to march miles outside the ghetto to reach the other jobs. There were workshops for carpenters, shoemakers, tailors and tinsmiths. After his Bar Mitzvah, my brother Berel went into a workshop. What did they teach him at the age of 13? How to be a *blecher*, a tinsmith. He learned how to make tin pails, cans, little boxes, and he learned how to solder the seams so they would be leakproof.

My brother caught on quickly. The way you solder seams is that you first apply acid, and then the hot solder bead follows the acid line nice and straight. He did such a good job that the supervisor accused him of not doing the work by himself because he just could not believe that a little kid who was new at this could do such perfect work. My brother started to cry and insist that he did it himself. Finally, he demonstrated how he did it. The supervisor was very impressed, and he made my brother an instructor.

For these jobs people were not paid, but they were given vouchers which they could exchange for food staples that were dispensed at various points in the ghetto.

Child in ghetto workshop

Child laborers in ghetto workshop

The Jewish Committee ran the show. They were responsible for the food rations, for supplying work details, and for making sure everybody in the ghetto followed the rules, which grew more stringent every day. Week by week, we were robbed of what little we had. At first we were ordered to turn over all domesticated animals and poultry, then all electrical appliances, then all books, then all pet dogs and cats – these were shot at the collection point – then all furs, jewelry and precious metals. Always the penalty for disobedience was death.

The Germans made frequent inspections, trying to ferret out who was trying to hide valuables. While searching on our street, they found a silver spoon half-buried in the sand. Nobody was trying to hide that spoon; it must have fallen there by accident. But they accused the man living nearby of trying to hoard silver, and they took him out of the house, put him up against the wall and shot him right then. My brother saw it happen.

If anyone transgressed, he was shot. And other people were made to come out of their houses and watch the execution. All this was to terrorize the Jews into cowering before them.

Weeks would go by and things would be quiet in the ghetto, and then the Nazis would come to stir things up. There would be another *aktzia*, another round-up. They would say they needed people for a work detail someplace else – Estonia or Latvia. In fact, some of these people were taken to a labor camp somewhere; others were taken to Dachau.

One day a truck pulled up in front of the ghetto hospital, and they went upstairs and started throwing small sick children – some only babies! – out the window onto the truck. By the time the truck pulled away most of those children were dead; they had broken their necks in the fall. The rest of the hospital, with the remaining sick inside, was set on fire.

I vividly remember – like it was yesterday – the first killing of a child that I witnessed. The Germans were going around, seemingly randomly banging on doors, doing "inspections," harassing people. I hid up in the attic, which was filled with raw wool for insulation. There, my father had squirreled away our most valuable possessions – the Torah scroll, some other holy books, and a few other valuable items (like saccharine, which was traded like gold). From my hiding place I saw, through a crack in the wooden siding, the soldiers dragging a family out of the house down the street. The woman had a newborn baby in her arms, and she was protesting – perhaps this was the offense for which she was being taken, because it was forbidden to give birth in the ghetto. Her protests enraged one of these pigs, and he grabbed the baby from her arms and holding it by the legs in front of her ripped it in two, as if he were killing a chicken. The woman let out a scream that must have been heard around the world, and she collapsed.

I do not remember the horror that I must have felt at this sight. What I do remember is the rage. I was overcome by rage, by the desire to kill, to avenge, to stop them.

I do not know why we Jews didn't do it. Why did we not rise up and overcome them? Today, if any people anywhere would be subjected to such inhuman treatment, they would riot and lynch the perpetrators. Why didn't we do that? We accepted it as if we had to. And we trembled like leaves. Why? Why were we so frightened?

Bar Mitzvah

It was in this kind of atmosphere that I had my Bar Mitzvah –
on Yom Kippur in the Hebrew year 5704 (תש"ד). My father very
much wanted me to *lein*, that is, read the entire Torah *sedra*, but
since it was Yom Kippur, the others would not agree that a 13-
year-old do it. He could too easily make a mistake, and this was
the most important holy day of the year. However, my father
convinced them to let me read some of it – the last section, the
Maftir, and the *Haftorah*, the selection from the prophets that
follows the Torah reading. In preparation for my Bar Mitzvah, I
learned with a tutor who taught me how to read the Hebrew
correctly, and he also taught me the proper blessings to say.

At this time, all the synagogues were already shut down,[40] so we
had the *minyan* in our house. My father unrolled the Torah scroll
which he had hidden in the attic, and that's what I read from.
Because it was Yom Kippur, a fast day, we did not have the
requisite Bar Mitzvah feast afterwards, but my father promised
me that we would have it a week later during the holiday
of *Sukkos*.

My father built a little *sukkah* in the garden – a little wooden
hut covered with evergreen branches – to celebrate the "Festival
of Booths." If the Germans had seen it, we would have been
shot, but my father, who was very careful otherwise, did not
compromise Torah. So we had a *sukkah*, and we celebrated the
holiday as best we could. My mother prepared a sponge cake and
my father brought out a little schnapps, and it was wonderful.

---

[40] One of them, the Veliuonos synagogue, was desecrated in a terrible way. Here all the cats and
dogs were brought to be shot. According to an eye-witness, "It was a cruel and sadistic spectacle:
wounded dogs and cats running about in the synagogue, wailing and shrieking." Their carcasses
were abandoned there to decompose over a period of months.

Imagine my surprise, decades later – when I was in my 70s already – picking up a book published by Harvard University Press, *Surviving the Holocaust: The Kovno Ghetto Diary* by Avraham Tory, and reading this story (about my Bar Mitzvah celebration) under the date October 13, 1943:

> This year, Rosh Hashanah and Yom Kippur were very sad days. Before *Sukkos*, however, the mood in the ghetto relaxed somewhat ... To celebrate the Festival of Booths some traditional huts were even erected, made from planks and covered in thatch. Even some citron (*etrog*) and palm branch (*schach*) decorations were found.
>
> On my way to the council offices [that is, the offices of the Jewish Committee] in the morning, I came across one such booth which had been erected near a large group of houses. This made me wonder about the Jewish will to live, which does not disappear, even in the ghetto. It seems that a sharp knife is at our throat, yet we do not lose courage. We do not cease being Jews...
>
> In the afternoon, I was urgently summoned to the workshops. Germans from the city governor's office were waiting there. Walking quickly to the workshops, I again came across a festival booth (a *sukkah*). Its door was open. Inside I could see a bearded Jew wearing a black hat on his head. He wore holiday clothes, and his face radiated joy. Several other people were in the booth with him. They were singing a chassidic song accompanied by the clapping of hands and the stomping of feet. They sang with devotion and enthusiasm, as if the ghetto and the German rulers did not exist.

The bearded Jew noticed me and came out of the booth. He took me by the sleeve and asked innocently: "What are you doing in our neighborhood at *Sukkos*? Peace be with you! A good and happy day to you!" He was in high spirits – even a bit tipsy. Probably he had drunk a glass of something to celebrate the festival. He did not listen to my reply, when I explained that I was hurrying to a meeting and was expected at the workshops.

"Have you eaten in a *sukkah* this year?" the bearded Jew asked. "No," I replied. "I have not had the time. Excuse me, I am in a hurry." The Jew – incidentally, a former Kovno merchant by the name of Zisman and an acquaintance of mine – looked at me with uncomprehending eyes, as if I were a heretic. He grasped me by the arm and dragged me into the booth. "Please come in!" he said in a resounding voice. I repeated my explanation: "I must hurry to a meeting affecting the whole community." But my reply failed to produce any effect on the bearded Jew. "Come in just for one moment," he said, and forcibly seated me on a bench inside the booth...

[Though I continued to object] Zisman was not deterred. He signaled his wife through the booth window; she responded instantly by coming in with vodka and cake in her hands. It turned out that the bearded Jew was celebrating the Bar Mitzvah of his son. He asked me to drink a glass of vodka and to recite the blessing thanking God Who made us holy with His commandments, and Who commanded us to dwell in booths; also the blessing over wine and bread. Needless to say I was asked to taste the cake. As we were eating, the Jews burst into song again: "If you say you are in trouble, the Lord's compassion will sustain you."

These words carried a special and profound significance in this booth in the ghetto. The Jews in the booth sang, with devotion and faith, of the compassion of God. I forgot myself and my mission, and joined the chorus and the faith. I was on tenterhooks nonetheless. But I could not leave the booth before I had fulfilled all of Zisman's wishes and observed the commandments. At long last Zisman said: "You have work to do on behalf of the community. We must not delay you." Seeing me off, he recited the traditional blessing: "The Lord will make you succeed; an errand of mercy is its own protection." He blessed me, wishing me to succeed in my errand and to bring good tidings, deliverance and comfort, so that we might be saved.

I arrived at the workshop late. The Germans from the city governor's office were waiting for me impatiently. I settled some minor matter with them and [continued with my duties of administering to the ghetto's many needs]. Throughout the day I remained under the good impression of the festive atmosphere in the chassidic booth. I admired those pious Jews and envied them their ability to set themselves free from the yoke of the ghetto, from the everyday troubles which keep pressing on each individual and on the community as a whole … "If you say you are in trouble," sing the Jews filled with faith, "the Lord's compassion will sustain you." Fortunate is the believer.

How did I come to read this book? A cousin of mine, Vivian London, who was a translator at Hebrew University in Jerusalem, read it in the Hebrew edition and saw something about our family. And she told me about it.

The author, who worked for the Jewish Committee in the Kovno Ghetto, kept a diary – day by day – recording everything that happened. And when he fled the ghetto before the *Kinder Aktzia,* which was the beginning of the end, he buried it. Immediately after the war ended, he returned, dug up the diary and had it printed. It has since been used as damning evidence in several Nazi trials.

In Hiding

As time wore on, people feared – knew, really – that the worst was about to happen, and they started preparing hiding places. They called these hideouts *malinas* – after the berry bushes that camouflage their fruits so well – in the hopes that when the Nazis came, they could not find them.

My father said, "How many times can we be lucky?" There had been so many *akztias* and selections, and with each one, we saw our aunts and uncles and cousins taken, and yet – somehow – our core family had been spared each time. But how long would it be before we, too, would be taken? So, my father decided we needed to have a hiding place.

Realizing that our neighbor across the street had the perfect setup for building an underground bunker – because there was a well and a shed close to the house – my father struck a deal with them to build something together.

Most ghetto houses had root cellars – cemented cubbies under the house or out in the yard where food could be kept from spoiling for an extended period of time – since most people did not have refrigerators. During the winter, ice taken from the river would be collected there, covered with moss or straw so it took a long time to melt, and that helped to keep the temperature low and to preserve food. We had one like that under the front of our house, and so did our neighbor. From his root cellar, we dug a 20-foot tunnel out to the shed where we created an underground hiding space of about 10-by-15 feet.

It took us months to prepare it. I remember carrying pails of dirt and spreading it out over the nearby fields so that people wouldn't notice. But, of course, people did; we were not really fooling anyone.

I think the tunnel and the bunker must have been below the frost-line, as we started digging in the winter, reinforcing everything with scrap lumber we had scavenged from around the ghetto. My father knew what he was doing when he built this bunker; he had thought of everything – water, air, light, toilet facilities, provisions.

The tunnel had a branch that went to the well – that's how we got the water. We removed the two top cement rings from the well, covered the well over and punched a hole into it under ground. We could lower a pail on a rope and fill it up. My mother baked toast, as bread would get moldy fast, and my father got a tin box to keep it in, as well as some sugar and a few other non-perishable foods.

Because there was no light in the bunker, my father had candles prepared, and he camouflaged a pipe to bring in air. In one spot, he dug out a big hole like a big bowl, so we could relieve ourselves. He had worked it all out – for someone who was not a professional architect, he made a splendid hiding place for us. That bunker was not made to last forever, but it was good for at least a month.

In late March 1944, the Jewish Committee heard that there would be a *Kinder Aktzia*. The Germans said that there were too many children in the ghetto, and they would take them to a place where they would be together with other children. They always gave an excuse when there was a *selektzia* – workers were needed in Estonia, or something like that – so there should not be a revolt. And people went along, because they wanted to believe this was so. They wanted to believe they were going to work and not to their death.

When my father heard that there was going to be a *selektzia* on the morning of March 27 – the 3rd day of *Nissan* 5704 (תש"ד) to be exact – he told us to get into the bunker. We all went down into the root cellar where a specially camouflaged entrance had been prepared, and then we crawled inside the tunnel on our bellies to the bunker. It was our entire family, and our neighbor's daughter, a little girl of about my age. I don't know why our neighbor did not go into the bunker with us.

We managed to hide out there for two days, but on the afternoon of the second day we heard knocking from the outside, "Everybody out!"

The Nazis knew there were bunkers and that people were hiding. So they caught our neighbor's elderly father, threatened to take him away and, to save himself, he pointed out the bunker to them. It was especially horrible because he also doomed his own little granddaughter who was hiding with us.

As we came out of the bunker, they immediately decided who they would take. They put my father, my younger brother, me and the little girl on one side, and my mother and my older brother on the other. What was the logic of this, I don't know. Later, it was established that during the *Kinder Aktzia*, they took old people as well as the children, and I guess that my father's beard made him look old.

As they were dividing us up, my father said to me, "Leibke, run!" He did not have to tell me this twice. I started to run. They could have taken their rifles and shot me, but they didn't. I guess they figured they would have a little fun, so instead, they sent a dog after me, a German Shepherd. I was a little boy and that dog looked to me like a pony, but with God's help, I managed to outrun the dog for about 400 feet or so. Then he got a hold of my pants. I was trying to pull away from him, when right at my feet I saw a fallen branch. I grabbed it and zapped him over the snout as hard as I could. He let go, and I kept running. He didn't chase me because, as I later learned, attack dogs are trained to return to their owners if their mission is aborted. But who can know the mind of a dog, or what God put in his brain at that moment?

I ran around the block and then ran back to our house and hid up in the attic. The Nazis came and searched. I was very quiet. Finally, they got tired of it, and they went away. I stayed there for a long time until my mother and my brother Berel came home. My father and my younger brother Chaim Yisroel did not come home. I never saw them again.

Berel told me that when they put my father and Chaim Yisroel on the truck, my mother ran after it, crying and pleading to let them go, but they forced her to back off. This broke her – she had been depressed before this, but now she was completely broken.

I heard later that they divided all the people they took – old people and children – into two groups. Some they took to a fort outside of town and shot over a mass grave. Others they put on a train to Auschwitz.[41] I do not know where my father and my brother ended up. I just know that they are dead. If my father hadn't told me to run, and if God had not granted me a reprieve, I would be with them today.

Last Days in the Ghetto

Afterwards, life was not the same. My father was gone. He had been the pillar of the family, the positive thinker who found a solution to every problem. My mother did not know how to go on without him; she walked about in a daze, a shell of a human being. She was not the only one. With most of the children gone, their parents were bereft. Whoever was still left in the ghetto was either broken like her or living in sheer terror. They all knew they could not possibly survive.

Yet, we still observed Passover. It came two weeks after the *Kinder Aktzia*. The Jewish Committee – which was disbanded right after – made the bakery *kosher l'Pesach* and gave out *matzos*. We made some kind of a *Seder* but it felt like a funeral.

As spring gave way to summer, we heard that the Red Army was advancing, pushing the Germans out. That is when they decided to liquidate the ghetto – on July 8, 1944 or the 17th of *Tammuz*, one of the saddest days on the Hebrew calendar, when invaders twice laid siege to Jerusalem prior to its destruction. On

---

[41] My brother Berel and I prefer to believe that they lived a few days longer, and we observe the anniversary of their death (*yahrzeit*) on the 6th day of Nissan.

that date, just a month before the Soviets marched into Kovno, the Nazis sent the 8,000 remaining Jews to their death.[42]

Some managed to hide out, and they set the ghetto on fire to smoke out the hold-outs, asphyxiating hundreds of people, but a few did manage to evade them. Not us though. My mother, my brother and I were taken. We were made to march from the ghetto across all of Kovno, escorted by the Gestapo while the Lithuanians watched, until we reached the train station at the end of Laisves Aleja. There, we were loaded up onto a freight train like cattle for the slaughter, and we started the long trip to our grave.

Our first stop was Stutthof – near Danzig, the port on the Baltic Sea.[43] That's where they unloaded us, and they separated out the women and the smallest children. My brother Berel was shunted to one side with the older boys and the men, while I, just 13-years-old, held onto my mother's dress. Then things happened very fast. Some desperate power seized my mother and, in that instant, she pushed me away from her very forcefully. She tore my hand away from her dress, and she said in a stern voice devoid of emotion, "Go with Berel. Go there. Go now!" I didn't want to – I wanted to stay with my mother – but I obeyed her. I was crying, but I obeyed.

Berel remembers her desperate cry in the midst of the melee, "Take care of him!" To this day, he feels deeply that she made

---

[42] These were the last remnants of the Jewish citizens of Lita – all the rest were dead by then, murdered by the Germans and their Lithuanian collaborators.

[43] Stutthof was the first concentration camp built by the Nazis outside Germany. It was located in a secluded, wet and wooded area west of the small town of Sztutowo, some 35 kilometers east of the Polish port of Gdańsk. More than 85,000 victims died there – in the gas chambers and from deprivation. Evidence was found at Stutthof that soap was produced there from human fat.

The ghetto was burned down after we were
taken away

Ghetto ruins

the mother's ultimate sacrifice. Rather than considering her own feelings and sheltering the one child who was clinging to her for protection, she gathered up all the strength within her to crush her motherly instinct and do the best for me.

I did not hear her last words; I was too bewildered to register everything that was happening around me. All I know is that I separated from my mother and went with my brother.

Now I understand that my mother knew she was going to die, and she was resigned to her fate. She had lost her husband and two children, she was broken, but she must have had some sixth sense that my brother and I still had a chance.

That was the last time I saw her. She was swallowed up in the crowd, and I have no memory of her face in that parting moment.

Berel and I were put back on the train and taken to Dachau, in Bavaria, Germany – specifically to a newly built sub-camp of Dachau called Landsberg. Here, unlike Dachau proper which had real houses, the accommodations consisted of A-frame wood barracks set deep into the ground, so that they were more like earthen huts. Inside, running down the middle was a long narrow aisle, and on both sides were three-tiered bunk beds made out of flat-boards. We were laid out like herring.

For two weeks, they trained us to become a slave-labor brigade. We had to learn how to march in step, how to take our caps off to a German, how to stand straight. We had to line up five in a row, in twenty rows, and God help you if you didn't start marching with the left foot. *Links, rechts, links, rechts.* Left, right, left, right.

Landsberg huts

After this training, they discarded 131 of the younger Kovno boys,[44] me among them. They realized we could not do a hard day's work like the older ones, and so, without making any announcements, they took us to a separate barrack, locked us in and quarantined us – not because we had any disease but because we were of no use to them – until they could put us on a train to our final destination.

My brother, who was 16, got to stay behind in Landsberg. He had a set of *tefillin* with him, and he gave it to me. HaRav Snieg, who was also at Landsberg, had managed to smuggle in his *tefillin*, and my brother said he would be able to borrow those, so I should have his. I took it along with my *siddur*, a picture of the

---

[44] The exact number is documented in Polish-language records I obtained, which list our concentration camp numbers and note that two boys out of the 131 died in transport. The date given for our Auschwitz arrival is August 1, 1944 – the very day that the Red Army liberated Kovno.

Rebbe Rayatz, and a little Jewish calendar (*luach*) that my father made me, showing when Shabbos and all the Jewish holidays came in. These most precious things to me, I hid in my big boots, which my father bought in just the right size.

They put us on a train to Auschwitz. This happened on *Tisha B'Av*,[45] the worst date on the Jewish calendar, when the Temple in Jerusalem was destroyed twice, and many other horrible things happened to the Jewish people. I knew this because I had the little calendar that my father made. On *Tisha B'Av*, 1944, the Nazis marked me for death, but God in His great mercy, let me live.

---

[45] In 1944, *Tisha B'Av* fell on July 29.

AUSCHWITZ

Auschwitz – the infamous concentration camp – straddled the Polish towns of Oswiecim and Brzezinka (renamed Auschwitz-Birkenau by the Germans after they annexed Poland). It consisted of various slave-labor camps, gas chambers and crematoriums, the latter concentrated in the Birkenau part of the camp. More than 1 million Jews died in this place.[46]

I remember well the train ride to get there. When we left Dachau, we (the Kovno boys) were packed into a freight car. But, of course, there were many more freight cars on this trip, carrying mostly Hungarian Jews, who were the last to be taken. I did not know who they were until I asked, and when they told me I had no idea where they were from, as I did not know European geography at all. I only knew that they were Jews.

It was a long trip, taking several days, though it should have taken a day only. I assume this was because the Germans needed the rails or the locomotives for shipments to the Russian front. So many times we were parked on a side track, waiting. It was the hottest point of the summer, the middle of July, and it was stifling in the cattle car which had only narrow openings for air, not big enough to stick a hand through. It was dark in there, and we mostly slept, huddled together on the floor.

Later I learned that they were using us as human shields. They were parking us between military trains to prevent the Soviet planes from blowing them all up. But they were wrong – the Russians didn't care about a few Jews.

Trapped in the freight car, not able to see out, we heard the planes whizzing above, the machine guns rattling. And they hit

---

[46] Auschwitz was a big complex of many concentration camps. There were three main camps, two of which were labor camps, and the third, known as Birkenau, was the extermination camp where the Nazis killed more than 1 million Jews and also close to 100,000 Poles and gypsies.

our train. We were lying on the floor, and there was a boy who was sleeping on my lap who was hit. I did not know it at first – because it was dark, and he didn't cry out. It was not until we had to get off, when I started shaking him to wake him up, that I realized he wasn't moving. And that is when I saw that he was dead. He had been killed on the spot, and because he died, I lived. His body had protected mine from harm. Only God knows why.

When I noticed that he was dead, I pushed his body away, and I thought no more about it. By then I had witnessed so much horror, so much death. I was focused solely on survival. Had I grown callous? I suppose so, but there was no other way to be.

Once the Russian planes left, the Germans opened up the train and told us to get underneath. I guess they felt this would be a safer place in case the Russians came back for a second round. But why? They were going to kill us anyway. Why did it matter to them where we died?

We got under the train. Right then we could have escaped but nobody did. If anyone tried, I know nothing of it. Of course I thought about escaping, but it seemed too risky. For one thing, if the Gestapo saw me, they would have shot me on the spot. For another, I was wearing striped pajamas (the concentration camp uniform) and was able to blend into the local countryside about as well as a zebra. I knew we were in Poland, but I couldn't speak Polish. So what good would it do to try?

After a while, they let us back up onto the trains, and we continued to our destination. Once there, they kept us on the train until nightfall. I was told later that this was so the people who came to the gas chambers of Birkenau should not see where they were going. They had powerful high-beams shining at us, blinding our eyes. They had thought of everything.

But what registered on us was the smell – a horrible, rancid smell filled the air – a smell we already knew well.

Unloading platform at Auschwitz-Birkenau

Crematorium at Auschwitz-Birkenau

As they were opening the wagon doors, the boys started debating if we should get out or not. One asked me, "Leibke, what do we do now?" So I said, "Let's march. Let's not go like sheep." Somebody said, "You really went off the deep end, Leibke. You're crazy." I got angry, "You asked me a question. I told you what I think we should do. If not, each one is on his own. Let's then say goodbye. Let's say *Shema Yisroel*.[47] And let's give up. I don't know anything else that we can do except what I just told you. I think that's what we should do."

Within a few minutes a few of the leaders – because I was one of the youngest ones – decided to do what I suggested. As we got off the train I said, "Let's go!" And all of a sudden I became the leader. "Line up. Let's do it right now." We lined up like we had been taught, in neat little rows, five abreast. I ran to the front, and we started marching in step, singing *Ani Maamin* ("I believe").[48]

I believe
With complete faith
That the Messiah will come,
And although he may be delayed,
Even so, I will await his coming
Each and every day

Marching like this, with the German guards staring at us stupefied, we made our way to the reception building. And there I said

---

[47] Jews are required to say the *Shema* prayer if they believe they are about to die.

[48] Why this song? We knew a melody particularly suited for marching, and it expressed our unquestioning belief in God, His Torah and our total faith in the Final Redemption. Of course, *Ani Maamin* ("I believe") is one verse of the "Thirteen Principles of Faith" authored by the 12th century Jewish sage and philosopher, Maimonides. As I later learned, this verse, which expresses the hope of a Final Redemption, was sung by many Jews going to the gas chambers and became known as the *Hymn of the Camps*.

in German, "Halt!" The guards went berserk; they were shouting at each other, asking: "What is this group? Where did they come from?" I guess marching like that we looked to them like the Nazi Youth or something. They were confused, and their leader was shouting for the papers.

But the papers were not there. By an act of Divine Providence, the papers did not arrive. Somebody lost them, or gave them to the wrong person. There were no papers. They did not know what to do.

As I came to learn, the guards at Birkenau were stupid; they were criminals, the bottom of the barrel of German society – any German who was a real man was fighting in Hitler's army; only the dregs got the job of exterminating Jews. Because their commanders did not fully trust them, they kept them on a short leash, and if one did the wrong thing, he was immediately executed. So they were scared of making a mistake which they might not be able to undo. And this state of things worked in our favor because, instead of taking us to the gas chambers, they decided to take us to the showers and to put us up for the night. In a sense, Birkenau was like a waiting hotel, where Jews waited to die because the Nazis couldn't kill them fast enough, and so they decided they might as well hold us over too. They could always send us to the gas chambers later.

They told us to get undressed. We were allowed to keep nothing except our belts and shoes. Not that we had anything. No one came from Dachau with a suitcase – you can be sure of that. But some kids did have a fork or a spoon or a picture. And, of course, I had my *tefillin*, my *siddur*, my calendar and my picture of the Rebbe Rayatz.

As we were getting undressed to go into the showers, we were told to throw whatever we had on a big pile in the middle of the room. There was already a big pile of things from our traveling companions – the poor Hungarians – who had been taken ahead of us. I was told to shake out my boots, and my most precious possessions ended up on the pile. That upset me tremendously. I said in Yiddish to my friends, "Fellas, we have to make a distraction, so that I can get my stuff back." And with that, I started a fight; everybody got the idea and joined in. The guards were taken by surprise, because just 15 minutes ago we were so organized, marching like soldiers and now, suddenly, we were fighting like wild beasts. There were only two or three guards there, and they tried to break us up. While they were busy, I ran back, grabbed back my *tefillin* and my other things and put them back into my boots. Then I yelled, *"Genug!"* and the fighting stopped.

Gypsy Camp

We went into the showers and afterwards got new striped uniforms. They sent us to *Tziganer Lager* (the "Gypsy Camp") which was a sub-division of Birkenau. Inside this vast complex, there were many barracks and sub-divisions, each holding about 400-500 people. Each of the subdivisions was called a *lager* (meaning "warehouse" in German), and was identified with a different letter of the German alphabet. These various warehouses of human beings marked for death were separated from each other by high wire fences; I guess to make it easier for them to control the prisoners.

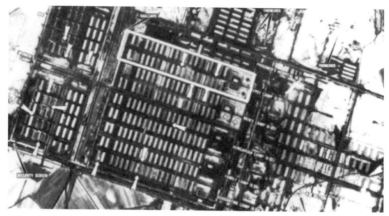

Map of Birkenau with Gypsy camp outlined

Barracks at Birkenau (interior)

Barracks at Birkenau (exterior)

In *Tziganer Lager*, all of us Kovno boys were put together in a barrack that had three-layered bunk beds all around and a stove in the middle (which, obviously, was not in use in the summer). In the morning, I put on my *tefillin* and so did those others who wanted to, though most of the boys did not come from religious families. We did it quickly, so everyone had a chance, as there was not much time to say the proper blessings and prayers.

Before long, word spread throughout the camp that someone had smuggled in *tefillin*, and other prisoners started coming around asking to use it. Years later, I read an account of this in the Hebrew work, *Encyclopedia Shema Israel*. This is how it was related:

Reb Chaim Toter showed up with a sensational piece of news – a *tefillin* and a *siddur* had been brought into the camp. His face aglow with happiness, he told us that, with his own eyes, he saw these *tefillin* in the hands of a Lithuanian boy who had arrived in the camp the night before. It was hard to believe that such a thing was possible. We all knew how many inspections an inmate went through before being allowed into the camp. Before showering, they would remove all his clothes, and afterwards he would exit from a different door, completely naked. And woe to him who had something in his hands. Reb Chaim swore that he was speaking the truth, and we had no more doubt that, indeed, there was a pair of *tefillin* among us.

The first to become enthusiastic about the news was Rabbi Yossele, the Rebbe of Novominsk, who rose and declared that tomorrow he must put on the *tefillin*. We tried to convince him not to endanger his life, because it would be akin to committing suicide. But the Rebbe proved to us that the concept of suicide does not apply to Auschwitz, "because it is like killing a dead person," and if the opportunity to do a *mitzvah* arises, one should do it, no matter what!

After we failed to convince or persuade him, we decided to forego the drinking of the morning "bitter waters" (otherwise known as coffee) and to hide the Rebbe while he put on the *tefillin*.

The next morning, when the bell rang, we gathered near Block S, where the Rebbe was already waiting for the boy, who was standing in the corner, adorned with the *tefillin*, and praying fervently. To my great surprise it was Leibele, the son of Reb Feivel of Kovno…

People waited and, through the little window of my barracks, I used to hand over the *tefillin* to others, among them, the Novominsker Rebbe. Of course, back then I didn't know who he was. Only much, much later I came across the account I have quoted here.

One day as I was at the window with the *tefillin*, a guard saw me. He did not see the *tefillin*, thank God, but he figured I was up to something. "What are you doing here?" he demanded, and I answered, "I'm just getting some fresh air." He said, "No, no, no. Who do you want to speak to?" I said, "Air, air, air." He didn't believe me. He came inside and grabbed me. He shoved my head into the stove that was in the middle of the room (which was not lit at the time), and he stripped down my pants. With his belt he started to whip me, demanding with each strike: "What were you doing at the window?" And I yelled back in German, "*Luft*! Air!"

When the Germans were punishing someone they wanted everyone else to watch – for the deterrent value – so all the boys were standing around, and some were crying, but I didn't cry. I was fighting back. In my *gingie* head something said that if I cried then he won. As long as I did not cry, I won.

He was hitting me so hard and so long that blood was gushing until, apparently, I fainted. Then he stopped hitting me. The boys got me out of the stove and put me on my bed. For a very long time – months, it seemed – I could not sleep on my back; I had to sleep on my stomach. But I had won. I still had my *tefillin* and I could still do this *mitzvah*, so it was worth it.

Human Horses

At *Tziganer Lager*, we had to work. Typically, we were awakened at six in the morning and given a black brew (ersatz coffee made from burnt wheat) and a piece of bread. Sometimes no bread, just coffee. After that, we went out to work. We were treated as if we were human horses. Instead of attaching horses to pull a wagon, the guards strung a rope and made two dozen kids pull it. We'd go from place to place – from Lager A to Lager B to Lager C – filling the wagon with garbage, taking it to the dump, and bringing the wagon back. We were the sanitation team. We did this the whole day.

Around us were barbed-wire fences as high as the eye could see. These were electrified so no one would think of climbing over. Besides that, there were watchtowers all around, manned by soldiers with machineguns. Yet, despite all this, they especially assigned one guard to watch over us little kids pulling the garbage wagon.

Auschwitz-Birkenau fence

Electric fence and watchtower

In this place, the roadways were not paved. They were just hardened clay, and when it rained, the clay could not absorb all the water, so there were puddles everywhere. And our guard liked to torment us – as if we had not been subjected to enough hardship and humiliation. He would stick his bayonet into a kid and push him down into a puddle. If a boy fell and got his pants wet, he didn't have anything to change into, so he had to walk around with wet pants.

One day I said, "If he does that again, I'm going to kill him." And, sure enough, he did it to a kid right in front of me. As I watched this guard with a gun hurting a scared little boy who could not defend himself, something in me snapped. It was just too much for me to bear. I said to him in German, "Why are you doing this, you pig?" The word "pig" – *schwein* – startled him. And, as he looked at me in surprise, I took my fist and hit him below the belt. I was weak, but he felt it; I had gone too far. Next thing I knew, his rifle was between my eyes. In my fury, I screamed at him, "Shoot! Go ahead! Shoot!" He didn't. As unbelievable as it sounds, he lowered his gun and walked away.

As I said, the guards at Birkenau were cowards; if they had been fit for battle, they would have been in the army. These people were the bottom of the barrel. Their commanders, obviously, were of a different class, of a different brand of evil, but the guards were German scum. I had humiliated him in front of the boys that he was supposed to be guarding, and he slunk away like a dog with his tail between his legs. But he could have just as easily shot me. It was a miracle that he didn't.

For a reason that was never explained to us, we were transferred out of *Tziganer Lager*. We lost our job collecting garbage. Instead, we were taken to a different section of Birkenau. Now, each day we went out of the camp, into the Polish town of Oswiecim, where we worked in the fields digging up potatoes. I guess they moved us because they needed more hands to gather in the harvest at the start of autumn.

When you harvest potatoes – especially in Poland where it can get very cold – you have to put hay on top of the ones that are not yet ready in order to protect them from the frost, which can come quite early there. For this purpose, big haystacks were already waiting in the field. I said to the other boys, "Listen, don't look for me. At the end of the day, come over to this pile of hay and holler, so I'll know when it's time to go back." I said, "I'm going to go dig myself into that pile of hay, and I'm going to relax and close my eyes. I'm not going to work over here all day without food and without anything, rain, shine or whatnot." And that's what I did.

So I went out with them, and I was counted, but once I was in the field, none of the guards noticed that I was gone. I was resting in the haystack. When it was time to go back, I was there for the final count.

Once or twice another boy joined me, but most of them were too scared because, if they were found sleeping in the hay pile, they would be shot on the spot. But I was wild, and my wild streak had not been beaten out of me; if anything, it had grown stronger. So for the larger part of the potato harvest, I lounged in the hay and ate raw potatoes. Raw potatoes are not mangos, but they are not bad if that's all you have. They have juice and a lot of vitamins, so they were a good dietary supplement for a kid living on black brew and a slice of bread a day. Of course, that dietary supplement came to an end with the onset of winter, but I had it through Rosh Hashanah until the bitter weather set in.

I remember well the Rosh Hashanah of 1944 because on the second day of the holiday, there was a *selektzia* in the camp. A *selektzia* sometimes meant they needed extra workers for a different labor camp, but generally, it meant they were weeding out the weaker workers.

Dr. Mengele[49] came, and everyone was ordered out of the barracks. We came outside and stripped to the waist. That was the procedure. Perhaps he wanted to see us naked so he could better decide who was worth saving a while longer and who should die immediately. He was also choosing people for his sadistic experiments of which I knew nothing at the time.

We lined up, and then we were ordered to walk past him. He had a thin leather whip that he kept in his high black boot, which was shined to a high polish. He used to take out the whip and point with it to the right or to the left. That was how he conducted the selection.

When it came to me, he told me to go to the left – the bad side. I said goodbye to the boys, thinking this was the end of the line for me. All of a sudden there was a big tumult – a soldier on a motorcycle came speeding down the main dirt road stirring up clouds of dust. He pulled up by our group and saluted Mengele. He said something which I could not hear, but it must have been urgent because Mengele immediately jumped into the side-car of the motorcycle and took off.

Now the guards didn't know what to do with us. They didn't know if the *selektzia* was finished or not. They didn't know if

---

[49] Dr. Josef Mengele, also known as the "Angel of Death," was an SS officer and a physician at Auschwitz-Birkenau. He gained notoriety for his selections of prisoners, which determined who would die immediately and who would be forced to work in a slave labor camp. He also performed sadistic experiments on the camp inmates.

Mengele was coming back or not. He hadn't said. They were arguing among themselves as to what they should do. In the end they decided that, instead of putting us on the truck and sending us to the gas chambers, they would put us back in the barracks.

That was yet another miracle when I could have died, but lived. I cannot explain it – other than that this was the will of God – that Dr. Mengele was called away at that very moment, and that the guards were fearful of doing the wrong thing. But that is what happened. They sent us back into the barracks, and that was the last *selektzia* that I remember. Shortly after the Jewish holidays were over (according to my little calendar), they stopped gassing and burning people. Suddenly smoke stacks stopped billowing smoke, and the people who worked in the gas chambers had nothing to do. As I later learned, the Red Army was advancing and was very close. The Germans knew they would have to retreat soon, so in order to conceal what had gone on at Birkenau, they ordered the gas chambers and crematoria destroyed.

At this time, they announced that anyone who wanted could go to a different camp to work. Some of the boys asked my opinion, "Leibel, what do you say?" I was against it. Since they weren't gassing and burning anymore, this place was no worse than any other, but at least we were familiar with it; here we knew what to expect.

However, not everybody listened to me. I do not remember how many went – 50 or so, about half of those left of our original Kovno group. It seems that only a few of them survived. The Nazis did not take them to another camp to work; they took them someplace else to die. They had many ways of killing the Jews. Auschwitz-Birkenau was one way. Dachau was another way. Treblinka was still another. There were concentration camps where they made people dig big graves and then undress and stand at the edge. There they would shoot them, and the people who were still alive had to push down the people who died but didn't fall into the grave. Then they brought tractors and covered the corpses with dirt. There are graves out there in Germany, Poland, Lithuania, Latvia, Ukraine, Russia where – in each one! – there are hundreds and hundreds of people buried.

I do not know what happened to those children who left at that time. When they went, I felt sad, as we all did because we had gotten attached to each other, and now half were gone.

Death March

We stayed at Birkenau until the middle of January 1945, when the Germans closed down the camp for good.[50] And those of us who remained – and there were thousands of people – were told to march. We marched. It was very cold, and we had nothing but rags to wear. After a couple of days of this, our group came to a train station, where there were freight cars waiting. They packed us in – not all of us, not everybody who was marching, just some. Others had to walk through the snow to Germany, and many, many died because they could not take the cold. I was spared that horrible ordeal.

The train brought us to the Mauthausen concentration camp in Austria. Mauthausen was a slave labor camp, and it housed

---

[50] Auschwitz-Birkenau was closed by the Germans on January 17, 1945, and 60,000 remaining prisoners were sent on a death march to Germany. The camp was liberated by the Red Army ten days later.

"political prisoners of the Reich" – especially intellectuals whom the Nazis intended to work to death. At that time I did not know this, of course, but what surprised me then was that there were so many non-Jews there. At Birkenau I hardly ever saw anyone who was not Jewish; here there were many Poles though I could not speak with them because they didn't know Yiddish, and I didn't know Polish.

Gates of Mauthausen

Mauthausen inmates climbing the "stairs of death"

But even though Mauthausen was not a death camp – without the horror, the terror and the smell of burning corpses – in my memory it was worse than Birkenau. At Mauthausen they took away my *tefillin*, my *siddur*, my Jewish calendar and my picture of the Rebbe Rayatz. I was separated from most of my friends, and I felt separated from my soul. For the first time, I felt lost. I didn't know whom to trust, and I saw there people betraying others just for a slice of bread.

I cannot judge them. They were starving. They were walking skeletons, nothing more. According to official reports, in 1945 the guards at Mauthausen issued one piece of bread a day for every twenty prisoners, and the life expectancy there was less than three months.

Time passed. It was cold in the beginning, but then spring came. It must have been around Passover time – April – though I cannot be sure because I no longer had my little calendar. We were happy to be outside in the fresh air after being indoors all winter. As we were standing in the yard, the Russian planes came flying over. We knew these were Russian planes because they had the red star painted on the underside of their wings, so you couldn't make a mistake. And then the bombs started dropping.

I remember the craters they made, and the splatter of blood and human flesh torn apart by their impact, the chunks of flesh landing against the barbed-wire fence that was everywhere around us. And then a horrible thing happened. Some of the people who were starving ran to the barbed-wire and started eating the flesh that was clinging there. They were starving, and they had become less than human; they had become like hyenas or vultures feeding on the dead meat.

The Germans had degraded the captive people to this level. They not only killed, they not only gassed and burned, they turned normal human beings into scavengers of human flesh. That was a horrifying sight, and the memory of it makes Mauthausen for me the worst concentration camp on earth – the very worst of all of them, because of the degradation that happened there.

In the beginning of May, they liquidated Mauthausen. They told us to march again. We walked from Mauthausen to a sub-camp at Gunskirchen. I do not know how long we walked; it seemed like days. Many people could not walk and collapsed; if they saw them, they shot them on the spot, while others were left lying there. As I passed a man dying in the ditch, he looked up at me and croaked out, "*Yingele* … don't forget me." I am so sorry today that I did not ask his name, but all the energy I had left was focused on trying to put one foot in front of the other; I had no other thoughts.

Those of us who made it to Gunskirchen were barely alive. We were housed there for the few remaining days of the war. We were given nothing to eat and nothing to drink. The Russians were coming from the east, the Americans were coming from the west, and the Germans didn't know what to do with us in those final days of the war. The last thing they cared about was these wretched creatures that they had brought to death's door.

A human being can live quite a long time without food, but only three days without water. To die of dehydration is a horrible death. I was so thirsty that I drank from a puddle in the gutter. I knew that I had to have some liquid, or I would die. I knew that. But this water was filthy. I cannot even imagine what this water was. And as a result of drinking that water and the ordeals that I had been through, I developed a high fever. I remember lying there and hallucinating. I had left this world and no longer saw the hundreds of dead bodies strewn about the camp, or felt the hunger, or smelled the stench, or noticed the insanity that was everywhere.

And then the Americans came in. It was over. Finally, it was over.

Liberation of Gunskirchen inmates

Later, I read a US Army report by a Lt. J.D. Pletcher on what they saw when they entered Gunskirchen:

As we entered the camp, the living skeletons still able to walk crowded around us and, though we wanted to drive farther into the place, the milling, pressing crowd wouldn't let us. It is not an exaggeration to say that almost every inmate was insane with hunger. Just the sight of an American brought cheers, groans and shrieks. People crowded around to touch an American, to touch the jeep, to kiss our arms – perhaps just to make sure that it was true. The people who couldn't walk crawled out toward our jeep. Those who couldn't even crawl propped themselves up on an elbow, and somehow, through all their pain and suffering, revealed through their eyes the gratitude, the joy they felt at the arrival of Americans.

I couldn't even crawl out. In the distance I heard shouting and singing. Happy sounds for the first time in such a long time. The Americans were there, and they were giving out food. People gobbled it down, and many died just from that. Their starved bodies could have coped with some soup maybe, but not rich chocolate or the other treats they were giving out.

But I was too weak to get any of the food. They put me on a stretcher and took me directly to the hospital, where they gave me liquids through an intravenous tube. And that's how I survived. Because I was sick, I could not go get the food that would have killed me. But the hospital personnel knew how to deal with someone in my condition. And I lived.

Kovno boys who were liberated from Gunskirchen (right to left):
me, Kalman Tsechanowski, Meir Gecht, Max Wolson (US Soldier),
Leizer Greis, Mordechai Levitan, Daniel Labanowski

LIBERATION

Shortly after the war ended,[51] I was released from the hospital and sent to a displaced persons' (DP) camp in Salzburg, the name of which I no longer remember (or perhaps never knew), along with many other survivors. I was 14-½ years old but I looked like I was 10.

At this time my birth date was changed. I was made one year younger, and my birthday became September 18, 1931. I do not remember how it happened. I guess someone must have looked at the calendar when I said I was born on Yom Kippur, which in 1945 fell around that date. Or perhaps someone Jewish picked this date out for me, since the number 18 is written in Hebrew as חי (*chai*) which means "alive."

I was alive, and I felt happy to leave the horrors of the past year behind me, yet I felt lonely. It must sound strange, but when I was in the concentration camps, I was so preoccupied with survival that I didn't think about anything else. Now that pressure was gone. I was free at last – free to go anyplace I wanted, but I did not know where to go or what to do. It hit me that, except for the few friends who were my age, I had nobody.

I knew that my father and my youngest brother were dead. We had never heard from my Bubbe or my sister, so I had no hope that they were alive. My mother? I didn't dare think. I hoped that my brother Berel had made it like I did, but I had no idea how or where to look for him.

In the DP camp, people were saying that it was best to go back where you came from. Somebody said to me, "You know, Leibel, you come from Kovno, so why don't you go back to Kovno? If

[51] Germany surrendered unconditionally on May 7, 1945.

your brother survived, he'll go back to Kovno. That's where you'll meet."

This advice made sense to me. But when I went to the DP camp office to make the arrangements to return to Kovno, I learned that there was a lot of red-tape involved because Lithuania was in Russian hands. At this time all the lands that had been recaptured from the Germans had been divided up by the Allies into four zones: American, Russian, British and French. And moving between these zones was not so easy.

Map of control zones created by the Allies

I filled out the necessary papers and waited. After a time, I and others who wanted to return to Eastern Europe were transported from the American DP camp to a different DP camp controlled by the Russians.

In the Russian Zone

When I moved into the DP camp in the Russian zone, I immediately realized that there was a big difference in how the victorious nations related to the survivors. In the American zone we had a lot of freedom. We came and we went as we wished, with certain small restrictions like a curfew. In the Russian zone, the camp was surrounded by barbed wire and guarded by police with guns. They watched us constantly. I knew I had made a mistake. But I did not know what to do.

Before I could develop a plan, I was called into the camp office. Sitting behind a desk there was a big guy, an officer of the Russian Army with red lapels. Apparently he was an administrator of the camp. Speaking to me in Russian (which I had learned in the years that Kovno was under Soviet domination), he verified my name and then asked me, "Do you know why you're here?" I said, "No, you called me. You tell me. I was just told to come in here."

He said, "I have read the statement you made on your application, and I have to ask you some questions." Then he began his interrogation:

"You say here you came from the Kovno ghetto?"

"Yes."

"You stopped off at Stutthof?"

"Yes."

"That was a women's camp?"

"Yes, that's correct."

"From there you went to Landsberg, a concentration camp?"

"Yes, it's true."

"From there you say that they separated you and your brother, because you were too young to work. Then they sent you to Birkenau."

"True again."

"You say they marked you for the gas chambers."

"It's true."

"But you're here!"

"I am."

"It's impossible that you could have survived all that. So, therefore, I have to conclude that you must be a collaborator of the Germans."

My reply was to spit in his face. It all just boiled over inside of me. I started yelling and cursing him. How could he accuse me of such thing after all I had been through?

He pulled out his revolver, and I started to shout: "Go ahead. Pull the trigger, shoot. Be a big man. Shoot a fourteen-year-old boy."

He didn't pull the trigger. He put it back in his holster, and he said, "You know, you're a lucky little kid. If there had been someone else in the room with us, I would have had to shoot you for what you did. However, I realize by your reaction that maybe I was wrong in making this accusation." In a way, he tried to apologize for what he said, and he offered me a cigarette. I refused it.

But I had cooled down a bit, and I realized that I needed to apologize to him for spitting in his face. I said, "I shouldn't have done what I did. I did it without thinking. It was a knee-jerk reaction, and I'm sorry for that." Then I told him, "You know, I have no way of proving to you that I was not a collaborator. I have no proof. I have nothing whatsoever, except maybe two old pairs of underwear. But I would like to demonstrate to you that I am not." I told him, "Next to this DP camp you have a big POW camp. The SS are housed there, also the Gestapo. I see that the Red Cross looks after them. If you would give me the opportunity, I would like to go to that camp and shoot as many of them as I can with one of your big Russian machine guns. After that you can give me an ice cream cone to eat, and I'll lick every morsel. I think that would demonstrate my hatred for the Germans in a fitting way."

He listened to me. And then he said, "You know, it's a novel idea. It's something to think about. In fact, the more I think about it, the more I would like to take you up on it and see if you really would do it. This way, of course, we would get rid of those Germans; nothing would please me more. And it would be a good reason to get rid of you, because it would show that you are not stable. You are a young kid who went through a lot, but sooner or later you're going to get into trouble because you react too fast."

"Well, why don't you try me? Let's do it. Call my bluff. See what happens."

But he gave me a reason why he was not willing to go through with the plan even though he liked it. He said he didn't trust me with a machine gun in my hands. I might not kill the Germans or

I might go through with it, but then there was no knowing who else I might kill. And that was the end of that discussion.

I went back to camp. To tell you the truth, at that time I didn't even think that anything big had happened. But it was a miracle that this Russian officer has not killed me for spitting in his face. They had a reputation for shooting people for less than that. Somehow God was looking out for me, protecting me, even from myself.

I continued to wait to be transported to Kovno, along with others who wanted to go back to Lithuania or Russia or Poland. And I was bored. There was nothing to do there. No work. No classes. The biggest event was dinner. They gave us bean soup, bread and coffee with sugar. That was our steady diet.

Until one day, they finally said, "You're shipping out tomorrow."

Under God's Protection

We boarded a train bound for Lithuania. Traveling was a long drawn-out affair, because the Russians were worse than the Germans; anytime they needed a locomotive, they moved us to a side track and left us sitting there. I noticed that the trains that were going by were transporting all kinds of machinery on open flatbed cargo cars. They seemed to be dismantling factories and industrial plants in Germany and shipping all that equipment to Russia. And that is why they needed the locomotives.

So we were parked somewhere in Hungary – Debrecen, as it turned out – under the watchful eye of Russian soldiers. But we were allowed to get off the train and stretch our legs.

As I was walking around I saw two young men – I'd say in their 20s – very well dressed in suits and ties. They had Jewish faces on them. So I asked them, "*Amcho?*"[52] This reference to "God's people" was the password for "Are you Jewish?" They turned around.

I was dressed in an old German pair of khaki slacks and a matching shirt, and I was wearing a little German cap. I was a redhead, so my fair complexion made me look more German than Jewish. They were startled by my question. I asked them again, "*Amcho?*" They said, "Yes." And we started a conversation in Yiddish.

When I told them I was going back to Kovno to see if anyone from my family survived the war, they were aghast: "Going back to the Russians? No, no. You don't know about the Russians. We know about the Russians. Don't trust the Russians." They became deeply concerned about my welfare, and one of them went to find out where our train was really going – it turned out to be Siberia!

They told me that if I wanted to find my family, there were lists of survivors available from the various Jewish organizations in Budapest. But I should not get back on that Russian train. I had no intention of it.

In order not to alert the guards, who might send out some kind of search party for me, they suggested that I should take my seat on the train until the passengers were counted, but once it started to move again, I should jump off. I could then hide in a wagon that belonged to them, in which they were transporting corn –

---

[52] Literally, "Your people." This term appears frequently in the Torah, for example: "Bless Your people, Israel..." (Deuteronomy 26:15).

kukoritza, as they called it. They unlocked the door to the *kukoritza* wagon, so I would be able to get in, and promised to come back for me in the morning.

I went back to the Russian train and told a Kovno friend who was traveling with me about the plan. I suggested he come with me, but he was afraid. He didn't know what to do. I said, "Well, you don't have much time to decide." As the train started to move, I asked my friend again, "Well, are you coming with me or not?" He said, "No." Sadly, I said goodbye.

When I jumped off the train, I hid between wagons until I could make my way safely to the one with the *kukoritza* and buried myself up to my neck in corn. And I waited. The Debrecen guys were true to their word. They came back for me in the morning and brought me to their apartment. There I took a hot bath, and they gave me clean clothes to wear, because what I had on I'd been wearing since liberation – which means I had it on me for three or four months already, and in the height of the summer there was a certain scent, shall we say, emanating from me.

I spent Shabbos with them, and when it ended, they gave me money to take a bus to Budapest. I am sorry I never wrote down their names because I would have liked to thank them properly. When they appeared, they were like angels to me, and they saved me from a terrible fate in Siberia.

Following their instructions, I arrived in Budapest and found the addresses they had given me – there were several Jewish organizations in the city helping survivors locate lost loved ones, but I did not find anyone I knew on their lists. One of these organizations put me in a homeless shelter, but the other Jewish kids there did not speak Yiddish, and I could not communicate with them. I felt like a misfit because of this and all the more lonely. Also, food was scarce in this shelter, so I didn't get enough to eat.

I remember I went wandering with another boy in a field outside of Budapest to steal plums off the trees – they were juicy – and we put them inside our shirts, so we would have something to eat the next day. We did that several times. Once we caught a little nanny goat, and we milked her, taking turns drinking right from her udders. (My grandmother would have been proud!)

I stayed in Budapest for the rest of the summer, until a few weeks before Rosh Hashanah 1945. During that time I got advice from another survivor that I should go back to the American side. At this time, Hungary was part of the Russian zone, and he said it was not a good thing to stay there. Survivors – because they'd had lots of training in this regard – were always alert and thinking on their feet; that is how they had made it this far. And they quickly realized that living under communism was like being in prison, while America meant a future rich with opportunities.

There was an "underground railroad" getting survivors out of Russian hands. They made me false papers of some kind, and along with a group of about 30 people in the same straits, we crossed over the Carpathian Mountains. We were trucked part of the way, but after that we had to go by foot, following an experienced guide along hidden mountain trails. We were climbing up and down the whole night, holding onto a rope, and I remember it as a fun experience. People were huffing and puffing, but I was enjoying the hike. When we got close to the border, the children were told to be very quiet and not make any noise so that we would not be spotted. We made it without getting caught.

My escape route from Budapest to Graz

Reunion

It turned out we had crossed over not into the American zone but into the British zone. We were in Austria, which was under British control. There, a truck awaited us and took us to Graz.

In Graz, there was a very organized DP camp – we got something good to eat morning, noon and evening, and best of all, the British were sticklers for record-keeping. On the wall, they had a complete list (constantly updated) of who was there, and they disseminated that list to other DP camps in Austria and Germany.

I spent Rosh Hashanah in Graz. And even though they had a nice meal with all the fixings and synagogue services, I felt forlorn, and this holiday – when we wish each other a sweet year – did not lift me up. After the joy of liberation, after the adventure of escaping from the Russians who wanted to send me to Siberia and destroyed my hopes of reuniting in Kovno with any surviving family or friends, I came to a realization that I could trust no one and that I was all alone in the world. This thought sent me into a deep depression.

It was during the days of repentance between Rosh Hashanah and Yom Kippur, when I was anticipating my 15th birthday and feeling particularly low, that I had a dream. The dream was extremely vivid – so much so that the people in it seemed alive as if I could touch them. In the dream I saw my father and my mother. They came to me and said, "Leibke! *Vos iz mit dir*? What's wrong with you? Don't you know that Berel is still alive? He's 17 now, and he's coming to get you. So, why are you giving up on life?"

When I awoke, I was very excited, because I knew that dreams come true. Had not my Bubbe dreamt about my father's arrest and rescue, and didn't it all happen the way she dreamt it? I was full of hope, but I didn't know anybody in Graz well enough to tell them about my dream.

It was the morning before Yom Kippur, when they called out my name on the loud speaker. "Leibel Zisman! Leibel Zisman! Please report to the office!" I didn't hear it at first. Then someone said to me, "Your name is Zisman, no? They've been calling you all morning. Why don't you go?" Then I heard it – they were announcing it in Yiddish, in German, and in Hungarian.

I went to the office and a lady asked me, "Are you Leibel Zisman from Kovno?" I said, "Yes." Then she smiled, "One minute. There is someone here who is waiting to meet you."

And in walked Berel dressed in a suit and tie and a little cap.

I ran to him, and we just started kissing and hugging. We were so overcome, we couldn't even talk. We were crying and hugging and laughing. The joy was indescribable.

When we finally calmed down, he told me how he had survived.

He had remained at Landsberg, the sub-camp of Dachau, for the entirety of the war. He was lucky that he got to stay there because he was the smallest of the slave laborers who were building a mile-long underground airport for the Nazis. Designed by Mohl, the famous German construction company, this was a massive project, a feat of engineering so huge that inside two planes could pass each other without touching.

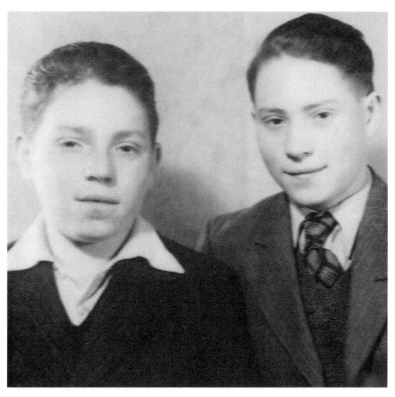

Berel and I shortly after our reunion

But it was back-breaking labor, involving cutting down trees, hauling lumber and, worst of all, hauling thousands upon thousands of bags of dry cement as endless trainloads arrived in Landsberg with supplies. He worked 12-hour shifts, and he was only fed a bowl of soup and a slice of bread twice a day. When his shoes wore out, he and the other slave laborers were issued wooden clogs to work in, and it was horrible for them because their feet got frost-bitten and were bleeding constantly. When a few people wrapped their feet in wool bits torn from a blanket, they were accused of destroying Reich property and hanged for this "crime" while everyone else was forced to watch.

Under these inhuman conditions people were dying daily, but my brother, though small, managed to brave through it. When the Americans entered Germany, the Nazis sent the inmates out of the camp, in staggered groups of several hundred each. They were marching on the road toward Switzerland and, at some point during the march, they told them to get off the road and lie down in the field. They went to sleep there and, when they woke up, they were covered with snow. Though it was April, it still snowed in the mountainous regions of Bavaria. They looked around and saw that most of the Germans were gone; they had run away. One of the few that were left told them to go to the nearest village, but they were afraid to budge. Then the *burgermeister*, the mayor of the village, rode out with a wagonload of bread and distributed it to the survivors. After they ate, they were invited to go to sleep in the hay barns of the village. (The villagers knew the Allies were coming, and they would be judged as Nazi co-conspirators, so suddenly they discovered kindness.) Before long, the survivors realized that the place was already being occupied by the Americans. They saw lots of tanks and armored personnel carriers with American flags on them. Then they knew that the war was over.

Berel was sent to Funk Kaserne, a DP camp near Munich. It was a huge camp, and all the people there were concerned with locating their loved ones. Every day lists of survivors from other DP camps were posted, and people would scour these lists for hours and hours hoping against hope. Berel did not find my name on any of the lists, but he heard from a woman who knew us from Lithuania that she had seen me in Salzburg. He was so anxious to be with me that he hopped on the next train in the direction of Austria. However, he found it was not so easy. As he tells it:

Berel's Story

"Although both Munich and Salzburg were in the American zone, Munich was in Germany while Salzburg was in Austria, so papers were required to go there. I could have gone to the Jewish Committee and filled out an application officially, but I didn't want to wait. I packed up a bundle and went. But when I got to the border, they took me off the train because I didn't have the correct papers. I was undaunted because I wanted to see my brother. I walked along the Salzah River, looking for a way to cross it. After walking a couple of miles, I found it. As I approached the town, I saw a guard booth and soldier inside. I scrunched down so he wouldn't see me. I was small, so it was not hard. I managed to circumvent the booth and get around to the other side, but now I was exposed. I devised a plan: I stood up and the soldier saw me. As I figured, he motioned that I couldn't enter. I pretended to give up, returning to where I had come from, except it was just the opposite, and now I was safely on the very road I wanted to take. I hitched a ride into Salzburg, and after much difficulty found the DP camp where Leibel was. Except everyone told me, 'Yes he was here, but I haven't see him for a couple of weeks … Yes, I remember him. I last saw him two weeks ago…'"

Though Berel looked high and low – and though many people remembered me – I was nowhere to be found. Of course, by then, I was either in the Russian DP camp, or on the train to Siberia, or already in Budapest. Distressed but glad I was alive somewhere, Berel went back to Munich.

There, together with a couple of Polish friends, Berel went into the ration business. While the German population was issued highly restricted rations, displaced persons could obtain as many as they wanted. This was because the Germans had to show identification and then be issued the ration cards, while displaced persons only needed to stand in line, and if they stood in line two or three times, they got a lot of extra cards. These they could trade for clothes – like jackets and shirts – or for cigarettes, which were more valuable than money.

Thanks to the ration business, Berel moved out of the Funk Kaserne DP camp and took a room in Munich with some friends, but he kept going back there every day searching the lists for news of me until he learned that I was in Graz. As before, he took off running without papers, but armed with a couple of clean shirts and two cartons of cigarettes. Again, I'll let him tell it:

"Crossing within the American zone was hard enough, but crossing from the American zone to the British zone was harder still. Fortunately, I learned that there was an underground railroad of sorts, hikers who would take you across. I arrived in Graz in the morning of Erev Yom Kippur. I arrived so early, the camp gates were still closed, but two packs of cigarettes got me in past the guard. Inside the camp, I found the Jewish section, and inside the Jewish section I found the Lita people. They knew who I was immediately, I looked so much like my brother. They said, 'Leibel's brother is here.' I waited in the office, and then in walked Leibel, 14-½ years old but looking like he was 10. I remember he was wearing a khaki shirt and pants that were several sizes too big for him held up with a length of rough rope tied in a knot. We could not stop hugging each other."

We spent Yom Kippur together and, right after, Berel said I should come with him to Munich. His DP camp was in American hands, and he thought that was the best place for us to be. We took the train, and Berel taught me the subterfuge of crossing between the zones.

In the end, we never went back to Munich because we stopped at St. Ottilien,[53] which was a DP camp near there. We made the detour because we heard that people from Kovno were housed there, among them HaRav Snieg, my father's friend who had been a chaplain in the Lithuanian Army before the war and who had been shipped to Landsberg with Berel. He had started a little yeshiva in St. Ottilien – about seven or eight boys – and he had some books of the Talmud for us to learn from. He was almost blind, but he knew the *Gemara* by heart. (Later he became the chief rabbi of Bavaria.) We got a bed there at St. Ottilien, and we studied for a time in his little yeshiva.

Meanwhile, we were writing letters to arrange our immigration to America.

Why did we want to go to America? We knew it was very hard to get to the Land of Israel (then called the Palestine Mandate) because the British who controlled it would not let Jews in. But, with relatives in America, we thought it would be possible to gain entrance there, and we also knew that the Chabad Rebbe, the

---

[53] St. Ottilien, a former Benedictine monastery, was a DP camp and hospital, headed by Dr. Zalman Grinberg, the former head of the hospital in the Kovno ghetto, and staffed with doctors and nurses who had survived the death camps.

Students at the St. Ottilien Yeshiva headed by Rav Snieg. Berel and I are the two smallest boys at the end of the table on the right.

Rebbe Rayatz, was in Brooklyn – this was an important thing to us, as he had been our father's Rebbe, and he had blessed us both before the war.

So, we wrote to him, saying that we were Reb Feivel's *kinder*, that we had survived, that we needed books to study, and that we were hoping to come to America. We sent the letter through a Jewish soldier in the American Army who spoke Yiddish. At this time there was no postal service from Germany to the US, so we gave our letter to this soldier who sent it via the US Army post. We did not know what the correct address was, so we just wrote: "The Rebbe of Chabad Lubavitch, Brooklyn." Miraculously, this letter got through.

Reb Moshe Leib Rothstein, the Rebbe's secretary, had known our father, and when he read our letter (as he told us later), he became very excited; he ran to the Rebbe to tell him that Reb Feivel's boys were still alive. The Rebbe was very happy at this news, and he told him to make a package right away and send us books and whatever else we needed.

ב"ה אסרו חג ה"ס תש"ו,
שיקאגא.

ידידי הרה"ג הרה"ח א"ח א
מוהר"ר ישראל שי' דו"קאבסאן.

שלום וברכה!

תמול הגיעני מכתבו של הבחור מר דוב בנו של ידידנו
ר' פייויל זיסמאן מקובנה. — יוכל היות כי גם כבודו יודע מזה, כי
קבלתיו ממשרד מרכז תו"ת, אבל מפפיקא הנני כותב גם לכבודו מזה.

הבחור דוב הנ"ל נמצא בקעמפ במינגען — אשכנז, ואחיו
צעיר ממנו נמצא בקעמפ, בעסטרייך בעיר גראץ, מכתבו נתקבל ע"י אחד
מאנשי חיל, אשר נזדמן אליו או שנמצא עמדו בקביעות.

מפכתבו גראה, כי רק הוא לבדו ואחיו נשארו בחיים מידי
הרוצחים ימ"ש, כותב כי מקוה כי עוד ימצא את אמו, אבל אודות אליו
ואחותו ועוד את קמן אינני מכיר, ממשפחת החמים פנחס מינץ (פיניע
אוזאריצער) שהוא דודו חושב כי אולי נשארו בחיים בתו חנה — הבלירה
כמדומני — מדודו אברהם (חמים) נשארו בן ובת.

בטח ידוע מקובנה כי זה פייויל זיסמאן הוא חתנו של החסיד
הידוע מקובנה ר' מענדיל ראסקין ז"ל, אחיו של פייויל דר בפילאדעלפיא
והנני רוש אדריסחו, כן מר לוי רצמאן הוא קרובי, וכמדומה שגם מר
פאשמאן הנגיד.

כמדומני שיש דרך להביאם לפה חמד גא ע"י השתדלות
הדרושה, ואולי יכול לעורר את מי מהקרובים להתעסק בזה.

כן נתקבל אלי מכתבה של העלמה פרת גיטא האבמאן היא
בתו של ידידנו החמים ר' יעקב הובמאן מדאקשיץ, כותבת כי נשארו בחיים
היא ואחיה מר משה ישעי' — למד זמן מה במילנא בתו"ת, ושואלת אודות
אבי' שעד פרוץ הפלמוח 1941 הי' בריגא, והנני רוש גם אדריסחו.

ידידו דו"ש ומכבדו כש"כו הנעלה

פ"ש מחתנו הרב ובתו הרבנית ונכדיו הילדה סימא והילד הערשעלע יחיו.

L. Zussman, 5211 Euclid Av. Philadelphia, Pa.

S/ Sgt. Harold B. Kalikow, (32394997)
741st Rg.opn.Br. A P.O. 350.
c/o Postmaster New York.

Гита Гохман
Энгельницкая ул. #5.
кв. Слободкина
Глубокое, Полоцкой Обл.

Reb Rothstein's letter conveying the Rebbe's wish to bring us to America

Reb Rothstein also helped us to make contact with our Uncle Leib (my father's older brother) in Philadelphia, and with our cousin Sima, my Aunt Tzivia's ambidextrous daughter, in the Bronx, and they immediately applied for visas for us in order to bring us to America. All that took quite awhile – a whole year really – and it was not till the end of 1946 that we actually got out of Germany and onto a ship bound for New York.

Meanwhile, we were tracking the various survivors who were arriving in Germany, and we found that some of our distant relatives (from our mother's side of the family) – all Chabadniks – had made it out of Russia by subterfuge. They were in a DP camp called Poking,[54] which was in the American zone and not far from us. So we decided to go there for Rosh Hashanah, arriving a week in advance.

We were hosted by the unofficial camp rabbi, Reb Nissan Neminov, whose wife was the daughter of Moshe Raskin, the brother of our grandfather, Menachem Mendel Raskin. That made his wife and our mother first cousins. They treated us very nicely, like family, like *mishpochah*.

We brought with us the books that the Rebbe Rayatz had sent us, and Reb Neminov was very excited to read them, especially the *Bikur Chicago*, a collection of the Rebbe's lectures. I don't think he slept for 24 hours, devouring that book, which among many interesting things says that we should recite the entire Book of Psalms on the Shabbos before Rosh Hashanah (which until then had not been the custom).

---

[54] The Poking DP camp was located in Waldstadt, Germany. Hundreds of Chabad chassidim were interned in the camp, which at its peak housed more than 7,500 Jewish inhabitants (many of them Russian survivors). It had several Talmud Torahs, including a Lubavitcher and a Klausenberger Yeshiva with a combined 500 students.

Immediately, he made an announcement to the whole camp that everyone should gather two hours before prayers and say the entire Book of Psalms. Afterwards, he explained why he made that announcement – that this was the Rebbe's decree which he had read in a book he got from us. So, we were the cause of a few thousand people at Poking reciting *Tehillim* on the Shabbos before Rosh Hashanah.

Now, before the High Holidays, it was the chassidic custom to submerge in the purifying waters of the *mikveh* – except this was a DP camp of survivors and the bathing facilities were scarce. Thousands of people were dunking in the *mikveh* and nobody took a shower beforehand. How can I describe the end result? The *mikveh* water took on a certain color and odor. It was not a pretty color, and the odor was not perfume. But I went in like everybody else, and afterwards – because, as so many red-heads, I had sensitive skin – I broke out in a terrible rash which turned into sores. I had picked up some kind of skin disease from somebody.

This skin disease almost stopped me from going to America. I knew I would not be able to obtain the clean bill-of-health that was a pre-requisite for being allowed to board the ship. But, fortunately, at that time Berel and I looked alike; we could pass for twins except that I had red hair while he had brown hair. So when it came time for the medical examination, Berel Zisman got the all-clear, and he turned around and went right back in line, but this time posing as Leibel Zisman. That's how I escaped from being put in quarantine and being made to wait forever for America.

We saw nothing wrong with our subterfuge – just the opposite. There is teaching from the Rebbe Maharash[55] (based on a Jewish saying, "if you can't go under a barrier, go over it") that when it comes to spiritual matters you shouldn't waste time trying to go under; immediately go over and move forward as quickly as you can. Well, I took this teaching to heart and applied it to every dilemma in my life, this issue with the skin rash being but one example.

The Long Wait

As it turned out, we had a long enough wait for America, and my rash had cleared up by the time we finally reached those golden shores. But in the meanwhile, we met a very special person – Rebbetzin Chana Schneerson, whose son had married one of the Rebbe's daughters (Chaya Mushka). She had heard that we were going to America, and she came to see us. She was still waiting for her papers, and she didn't know when she would be permitted to travel. (She didn't know then that her son would come to Europe to escort her home himself.) She had a slow, soft way of speaking. She asked us if we would be so kind as to take a letter to her son. We asked, "Who is your son?" She said, "His name is Menachem Mendel. You'll ask at the Chabad headquarters. Over there they'll point out who he is." Of course, we agreed. We had no idea then who she was introducing us to, or that her son would become the next Chabad Rebbe.

---

[55] Rabbi Shmuel Schneersohn (1834–1882), known as the Rebbe Maharash, is famous for saying: *Lechatchile ariber* — "immediately go over."

At Poking, we also met some other young chassidim who urged us to spend Yom Kippur with the Klausenberger Rebbe[56] at a nearby DP camp called Föhrenwald. We agreed because we were intrigued by what they said to us: "Before you go to America, come spend Yom Kippur by us. You'll see something different."

It sure was different. We never before saw these kinds of people with long side-locks (*peyos*), beards and black hats. In Kovno, where there were many chassidim of various persuasions, there were no Klausenberger chassidim that I could remember, and the rest of the religious Jews were regular Ashkenazim. Although our father had a beard, most of the people we saw did not. Of course, by Torah law you cannot shave with a razor, but you can cut your beard with scissors or with an electric razor which uses a scissor-

Klausenberger Rebbe's yeshiva at Föhrenwald

---

[56] The Klausenberger Rebbe was Rabbi Yekusiel Yehuda Halberstam (1905-1994). He grew up in Romania near the town of Sanz, where he was known as a child prodigy and great scholar. At age 23, he became the rabbi of Klausenberg, where he attracted a great many followers, nearly all of whom were wiped out in the Holocaust. He himself lost his entire family. He emigrated to America in 1947 and later moved to Israel, where he founded the community of Kiryat Sanz near Netanya, as well as the Laniado Hospital there.

like action, but this was before electric razors were invented; everybody then used a chemical – a depilatory – which could burn your skin if you left it on too long. Most of the religious Jews we knew did not have beards, but all the Klausenberger chassidim did. And also when they prayed they were very loud. Chabad chassidim prayed quietly, inside. But these guys were wild – they jumped up and down, shouting, hollering. I had never seen anything like it.

Also, I had never heard anyone like the Klausenberger Rebbe, who was a very powerful speaker. He was young at that time, in his early 40s. He had lost his whole family and almost all his followers in the war, and I still remember some of what he taught on Yom Kippur that year, because he had me and everybody else in tears. Thousands of people came to hear him speak, and all were crying like babies.

He said, "Why do we wear white on Yom Kippur? What is the significance of white? In the Jewish tradition, the groom wears a white robe (*kittel*) on his wedding day and his bride wears a white dress to show they are starting fresh, that they are pure. Also when people die, they are buried in white shrouds for the same reason. And on Yom Kippur, we want to show that we are pure, that our souls are without the stain of sin, as white as the driven snow because we have atoned for all our wrongdoings. Also on Yom Kippur we remember the dead when we say *Yizkor*, the prayer of remembrance. We remind ourselves of the white shrouds that our deceased parents and grandparents wore when they were buried." And then he paused, and his voice cracked, "Except that our parents were not buried in white shrouds ... Our parents, our grandparents, our brothers and sisters were buried in rags, their bodies mangled in mass graves. So why do we wear white?! They did not go to their judgment in white! If this is meant to remind us of our deceased loved ones, let's look like them!" And with that, he tore off his white *kittel*.

And everybody started to sob. He could not control the crowd. All the people – not too many of whom had *kittels*, after all where could you get one in a DP camp – were crying their eyes out. He said that we should not cry; anyone who had survived the war was holy, was pure, and did not need to put on white. But the people kept on sobbing; he had opened the floodgates, and nobody could stop the outpouring of pain that day.

I am sorry that I cannot capture his words nor the emotion of the moment. I am just giving a short summary. It was an unbelievable experience. Everybody was sobbing uncontrollably. I was sobbing. The Rebbe was sobbing. The floor was wet with tears. It was a moment I will never forget.

I also remember that before Yom Kippur, his *gabbai* came to him and told him, "Rebbe, there are children outside who are crying because they have no mother or father to give them the traditional blessing – the *birchas habonim*." And when he heard that, he called them in and he blessed them all, one by one. It was so beautiful, because he had lost his entire family, all his children – eleven of them.

Sailing to America

Sometime after that Yom Kippur we went to Bremenhafen, the port where we were supposed to board a boat for America. But, because of a sailors' strike, we didn't get on it.

After all the anticipation we were told we were not going anywhere. "Why not?" I asked. "There's a strike," came the answer. Needless to say, I did not understand what a strike was. When they told me there were no workers to man the ship, I said, "What do you need workers to man the ship for?" They explained that, in order for the ship's engine to operate, coal was necessary. Workers had to shovel coal constantly into the furnace so that the heat would make steam and give power to the motor. If there are no workers to do that, nothing would move. "Then get other workers," I said. "There are so many of us who want to work. I'll do it. I want to get to America – I'll do it." But they said, "Not possible. The union won't allow it." The union? I had so much to learn.

So we sat in the port waiting. The Klausenberger Rebbe was also there waiting to board the same boat, and we joined him and his students. We bunked a dozen boys to a room, and for a change we didn't mind the crush.

The Klausenberger Rebbe was famous, so people came and brought him food, and being close to him, we benefited. I remember one Shabbos when he invited me to sit on his right side because I had a good voice, and he liked to sing. He was singing *Shalom Aleichem*, the opening song before the meal, and he was singing and singing – for a half-hour it seemed like to me. I participated as long as I could, but I was hungry, so I stopped. I went into a side room and made my own *Kiddush* (the blessing over the wine), and then I came back and started to eat. In the middle of singing, he turned to me and said, "Leave something for me!"

After this, we became good friends. We spent eight weeks in one room, waiting for the boat, then another two weeks on the boat. Through all this, we got to know each other well – after all, we slept, we ate, we learned, we prayed and we played together. While we were still in the Bremenhafen port, I got him to play chess with me. I was 16 years old, and I just couldn't learn Talmud from morning to night. So I found a chessboard and asked him if he wanted to play. He said, "Fine, but first we'll learn *Gemara*, and after that we'll play chess." I agreed, and that's what we did.

The Klausenberger Rebbe

I liked the Klausenberger Rebbe a lot; he was a very impressive man, though I knew he could not be my Rebbe, because my father told me that we were Chabad Lubavitch and my Rebbe was the Rebbe Rayatz. I felt I was one of his favorites though. For example, he used to learn deep into the night, until 1 or 2 in the morning, studying the *Gemara* by candlelight. He tried to get us to keep up with him but we were only human; we would nod off and our yarmulkes would fall off our heads. So he'd put them back on and try to wake us up. When he did it to me, I asked him, "What is the difference between hitting me with a rock on the head and hitting me with the Talmud on the head?" And he said, "What do you mean?" I answered, "All night long you are hitting me with the *Gemara*, and you won't let me sleep." When he heard that, he laughed. I am mentioning this only to show how close we became – I was close enough to him to be able to joke around with him.

Finally, after two months, the strike ended, and we boarded the boat. Now, this was not the Queen Mary; it was more of a banana boat – a *small* banana boat at that. The water was rough in the Atlantic in the winter – we were making the voyage at Chanukah time – and from the second day out on the ocean, I was seasick. It was a very, very rough trip. And it took two weeks to cross the Atlantic in this thing because we went about three miles an hour. It was up and down with every bump and every wave. We were lying on the floor for most of that time. I said, "Good thing they didn't take me up on my offer to shovel coal. Because right now the boat would be standing in the middle of the ocean while I was up-chucking my dinner."

The Klausenberger Rebbe was trying to recruit boys for his yeshiva, and he wanted me and my brother to come learn with him, but we said that we were committed already – we were going to Brooklyn, to the Chabad Lubavitch headquarters at 770 Eastern Parkway.

After a while he realized that we were Chabad through and through, and going with him was just not in the cards for us, but he made us promise to come visit him. Once we got to New York, we visited him every Thursday night for about two years. We used to go on the Kingston Avenue trolley car to Williamsburg – which cost one or two cents then and ran on rails – and we would come there late at night. He always greeted us very warmly, asked us what we were learning, and gave us treats. He usually had a big bowl of fruit in the middle of the table – and that's all that my hungry eyes needed to see. He'd say, "Make a *brocha*." And I would take an apple, make the requisite blessing, and inhale it. So he'd say, "Take another." Then he'd say, "Take some home." I would put all I could in my pockets, and open up my shirt and stuff all I could against my chest. His new wife, the Rebbetzin, would come in and ask, "What happened to the fruit? There was so much here." And he'd wink at me and answer, "Somebody must have taken it. I remember it was full, and now it's empty. Please bring more." And when she went out, he'd burst out laughing.

He was wonderful. He was our friend. And I was sorry when he emigrated to Israel, though he did great things there, establishing a whole chassidic community and the Laniado Hospital in Netanya; I missed him.

But I am getting ahead of the story.

BROOKLYN

When we arrived in New York, there were lots of people there to greet us – as if we were dignitaries.

The Rebbe Rayatz sent a welcoming committee to the docks – he was so moved that we were the only survivors of the entire Chabad community in Kovno.[57] Despite his stature and efforts, the people from the JOINT (the American Jewish Joint Distribution Committee), who were managing the refugees, would not release us to his care. They said they were sorry, but we had to stay in their custody because we were under age – my brother was 17 and I had just turned 16 when we arrived – until our future could be determined by the proper authorities.

Also waiting to greet us was my Uncle Leib (now called Lou), one of my father's older brothers who had been living in America for many years. He and the other brother Yosef (now called Joe) were the closest living relatives we had. Uncle Lou asked us, "Where are your suitcases?" We said, "What suitcases?" We had nothing to bring, as our worldly possessions consisted of a change of underwear, our *tefillin* and the books that the Rebbe had sent us. This we had in a little hold-all, which was about as big as a purse. HaRav Snieg at St. Ottilien had given us $5 each for the journey, and I pulled out the bill to show Uncle Lou; I said, "Don't worry. We have money." God bless him, he didn't laugh.

Uncle Lou was not permitted to take us either. Instead, we were sent to a little hotel near the docks in the East Bronx where we were quarantined until we could pass all the health checks, and it could be decided where we should go.

---

[57] We learned this later from the Rebbe's secretary, Reb Rothstein.

As it happened, our cousin Sima, who had married Reb Avrohom (Abe) Jacobson,[58] was living in the West Bronx, and despite the quarantine, she wangled special permission to have us over for Shabbos meals. Since we arrived late on Friday, in order not to desecrate the holy day, Sima and her husband had to walk in a snowstorm to escort us to their home, which was near Yankee Stadium and nowhere near the docks. It was a two-hour walk one way across the entirety of the Bronx, but they didn't seem to mind. From Sima's entire extended family, only one sister – Nechama[59] – had survived, and Sima was overcome with joy to see us.

Sima and Abe   Their daughter Vivian

[58] See note VII in APPENDIX for additional details.

[59] Nechama married Nathan (Nochum) Gutwirth, a Dutch boy who was a student at the Telz Yeshiva in Lithuania. Because Nochum was a Dutch national, they were able to get permission to migrate to Dutch East Indies (Indonesia). Unfortunately, Indonesia was captured by Japan and they were imprisoned, but when the war ended, they were able to make their way to New York and moved in with Sima.

Sima and Abe's daughter, Vivian, who was eleven at the time, remembers the fanfare surrounding our arrival, especially that her mother made *cholent* for the first time. Of course, Sima knew that my mother always made *cholent* for Shabbos, and so she went to all that trouble to make us feel at home.

When we sat down at the table, they wanted to know everything that had happened to us, and Berel talked up a storm, telling them the story.[60] They knew that millions of Jews had been murdered, but they had no idea about the horror of the camps. Berel described it all in detail, but I said nothing. Vivian remembers that I didn't speak at all and that my eyes were constantly flitting from face to face and from wall to wall. Truth be told, I didn't trust them. They seemed like nice people, but nice people had lied to me before; nice Russians had told me I was going to Kovno and put me on a train to Siberia. So was this really America? Was this really New York? I was taking it all in; I had been through too much to open myself to anyone, not until I was sure I was truly safe.

We stayed over in the Bronx hotel for a week or so, until the authorities were satisfied that we would be in good hands, and they released us to the care of the Chabad Headquarters at 770 Eastern Parkway, Crown Heights, Brooklyn.

In 1940, when the Rebbe Rayatz arrived in the U.S. from Russia, he acquired 770 – a big three-story brick building, which had once been a hospital. He lived there in an upstairs apartment

---

[60] Once she heard in gruesome detail what they did to us, Sima, who was an accomplished multi-linguist and quite proud of her skills, stopped speaking German. She could not. Her daughter, Vivian, remembers well that she never uttered a word in the German language to the day she died.

Chabad Headquarters at 770 Eastern Parkway, Crown Heights, Brooklyn

(descending in an elevator in his wheelchair); the *shul* was also there, and a small yeshiva for about two dozen advanced students.

When we walked through the door, we must have looked like we came from Mars. We looked strange, but everyone else looked strange to us. We were clean shaven; they had beards. We wore colored hand-me-downs; they wore basic gray. (In those days, all Chabad chassidim in Brooklyn wore gray; even the Rebbe wore gray during the week, changing into black suit, hat and white shirt only for Shabbos.)

Meeting the Rebbe

We had the letter from Rebbetzin Chana Schneerson, so first of all we asked to see her son, Rabbi Menachem Mendel Schneerson, who was the son-in-law of the Rebbe Rayatz and not yet the Rebbe (he would assume leadership in 1951 after the passing of the Rebbe Rayatz). He was pointed out to us. I remember that he wore a double-breasted gray suit and a gray hat with a black band. We spoke to him in Yiddish, and we gave him the letter from his mother. He opened the letter and began to read it. From what I could see, it was not a long letter, but he took a long time with it. Too long, it seemed to me. I finally said to Berel, "What is he reading so much?" I did not understand that this letter was precious to him, as he'd had no communication with his mother for years.[61]

Finally, when he finished, he turned to me and asked, "How does my mother look?" And I answered him, *Vee ahn alte yiddene.* ("Like an old lady.")

He smiled and said, "Could you describe her?"

Note that he did not ask Berel, who was obviously older, but me with the wild look and no inkling of diplomacy. He probably heard me mutter about the length of the time he was taking with her letter, and I think he felt that from me he would get the unvarnished truth.

As it happened, I had a photographic memory when I was young – I could see a picture in my mind and be able to give it

---

[61] The Rebbe's father, Rabbi Levi Yitzchak Schneerson, was arrested in 1939 by the Soviets for Jewish activities in Russia. After more than a year of torture and interrogations in Stalin's prisons, he was sentenced to exile in a remote village in Kazakhstan. After he passed away in 1944, Rebbetzin Chana was able to move to Moscow, and there obtained a false passport to leave the Soviet Union. She arrived in Germany, was housed at Poking, then made her way to Paris, where her son met up with his mother for the first time in 20 years and brought her back with him to New York.

over. Even to this day, I can walk into a house, walk out, and describe exactly what I saw, even draw a diagram if need be. So I told him what he wanted to know – that she seemed very thin and pale, that she spoke softly, and that she wore a long blue dress with flowers on it and a *peruke* ("wig"), but no make-up or lipstick.

He didn't seem to get enough of it, and he peppered me with questions for half an hour. When he had exhausted my recollection, he thanked me, and then he went to the bookshelf and took down two books – *Likutei Torah* – and he gave one to me and one to Berel.

As we were going out the door, he called me back and said, "When you need something, you come to me." And that is how my relationship with the Rebbe (who wasn't yet the Rebbe) began.

The Rebbe when I first met him (when he wasn't yet the Rebbe)

After this, we had an audience with the Rebbe Rayatz. Reb Rothstein who brought us into his study gave him a note which explained who we were. But he pushed the note away, saying, "I know very well who they are," and he sent Reb Rothstein out of the room.[62] He waited until the door clicked shut, and he looked at me. It was the same look that he gave me in 1939, back in Riga. His eyes pierced through me like x-rays. Even though I was a wild kid who had stood up to Nazis and Russians, I started shaking, just like I shook in Riga. And I was just as scared.

Then he started to ask us questions. He wanted to know exactly what had happened. So we explained to him about the ghetto, about the *Grois Aktzia* and about the *Kinder Aktzia*. We told him about our father and about our younger brother, about what happened to our whole family and to the whole Chabad community in Kovno. He asked us many questions, and he was particularly interested if certain people had survived. And little by little, he confirmed that nearly everyone was gone. And then he started to cry.

He was sitting in his wheelchair, sobbing, his whole body shaking, and we were crying with him. Reb Rothstein must have heard through the door and knocked, but the Rebbe didn't answer.

After a while, he composed himself. He told us we had a place in the Chabad yeshiva, gave us a *brocha* and at last called in Reb Rothstein, whom he instructed to take us to see his wife, Rebbetzin Nechama Dina, so that she would give us *sukarkes* (the same hard candy that his mother had given us back in Riga).

---

[62] Reb Rothstein later told me that, when the Rebbe Rayatz heard that Shraga Feivel Zisman's kids were coming, he put on his *spodik*, a tall fur hat he only wore on Shabbat, holidays and for public appearances. He did this especially, I feel, to honor my father's memory.

We were taken to the second floor to their apartment – which was furnished in an aristocratic style. I remember a long table, in the middle of which stood a big crystal bowl filled with candy in colorful wrappers. There must have been five pounds of candy in that bowl – I had never seen so much candy.

The Rebbetzin had difficulty hearing, so there were two ways of communicating with her. You could look at her face-to-face and speak slowly so she could read your lips, or you could write down what you wanted to say on a clipboard. Reb Rothstein had a clipboard, and he wrote something for her to read. I imagine it said: "Please give *sukarkes* to these poor kids!" And she started to holler, "*Kumt kinderlach, kumt kinderlach!*" Her voice was so loud, I'm sure you could hear her on the other side of Eastern Parkway. Then she started to scoop up the candy with both hands and fill our arms with it, as much as we could hold.

From there, we were taken to the yeshiva dormitory – which was located some distance away from 770 – where we were given beds. But after a few days, we asked for a private place. We said, "We are grateful and everything, but we just finished years of concentration camps and DP camps, and months of waiting for a boat with a dozen people in one room. It feels to us like we are changing countries but our situation remains the same – we are still in one room with ten people. Can we be on our own please?"

They understood and they agreed, even though it meant going against their rules. With the help of Sima – who had us over every Shabbos – we found a room with the Gutkin family on Lincoln Avenue. (Gedaliah Gutkin was a *kosher shochet*, and he later taught me how to slaughter chickens in the proper way.) We slept there only; every morning we came to the yeshiva – to pray, to eat, to learn – and we only went back after supper.

Special Treatment

This was one of many exceptions granted me and Berel because of what we had been through, and also because we were serious students. When the other boys went home, we continued to learn; we had nowhere else to go. Later we learned that the Rebbe Rayatz had told the teachers to treat us with special sensitivity and to make exceptions for us. There were a lot of things that we did that were not exactly within the guidelines of Lubavitch – for example, in the early years we shaved. Later, after he got married, Berel decided to grow a beard, but I didn't, even though most of the young men in the yeshiva had beards. Yet no one said anything to me, nobody ever criticized me, and if anything, everybody treated me as special. From early on I sensed that I had privileged status.

In the first few years (1946-1950) in Brooklyn, I always managed to squeeze into the special *minyan* that accompanied the Rebbe Rayatz in his Rosh Hashanah and Yom Kippur prayers. Being wheelchair-bound, the Rebbe prayed upstairs in his study as he could not descend on the holiday via an electric elevator to the main *shul*, and about a dozen senior chassidim prayed in an adjoining room with the connecting door open.[63] Of course, his son-in-law, the future Rebbe, was there and, as he came up the stairs, many people eagerly waited to see if there was perhaps space for a couple more to enter. I usually elbowed my way up the line and, as he was opening the door, he would hold it open and motion for me to slide in. From the time that he said to me, "When you need something, you come to me," I felt he was looking out for me.

---

[63] See note XII in APPENDIX for additional details.

On another occasion, on Simchas Torah, Berel and I found ourselves walking past 770 at 1 o'clock in the morning. The dancing had taken a long time, the meal after had taken a long time, but there were still a few stragglers left hanging around. We poked our heads in and saw that the future Rebbe was there with a few people. He greeted us warmly and explained who we were to the others, "These are Reb Feivel Zisman's *kinder*." And then he invited us to join him in a *l'chaim*. One of the others produced a bottle of vodka but no glasses could be found. So we all drank using the little bottle cap as a vessel, and I remembered what my father had said to the Rebbe Rayatz so many years ago on Simchas Torah in Poland, "May I have the vessel as well as the light?" But on this occasion, there was no crystal shot-glass for me to pocket.

At this time, we were learning in Chabad's Bedford Yeshiva, which was for high-school age boys; only the older fellows learned in the main yeshiva at 770. The Bedford Yeshiva was a multi-story building, which consisted of a *shul* on the ground floor, the classrooms on the second, and the dormitory on the top. Some eighty boys learned there – Torah and Talmud in the mornings, secular subjects (history, geography, math, English, etc.) in the afternoon.

Rav Mordechai Mentlik was the head, the Rosh Yeshiva; Rav Eli Moshe Liss was the custodian (*mashgiach*), and it was his job to make sure everybody got to class on time, prayed on time, learned on time. He used to pull our ears if we didn't behave. But even though he was strict, the boys liked him because he was so sincere – we felt he truly cared about us. If somebody didn't feel well he fretted like a mother hen until the boy got better. If somebody was homesick, he was there with a kind word. And he took care of our personal needs – buying us shirts and shoes and hats – as well as our learning.

In the beginning I was very quiet. I hardly spoke. Sima was so worried about me – fearing that perhaps I had been psychologically damaged by my experiences – that she sent me to a psychiatrist. But I didn't tell him any more than I told everybody else, which is to say I told him nothing. I could not have put my feelings into words even if I had wanted to. I was full of guilt and rage. I kept asking myself, over and over: Why did we all go like sheep to the slaughter? Why didn't we rebel? Why did we cooperate in our own destruction? And most of all, I kept asking myself: Why didn't I do more? (As if I could have done more and didn't.)

All these roiling feelings came to rest inside me – inside one small person. I picked street fights with random people whom I perceived as bullies or anti-Semites, until Berel told me to stop it. He saw me coming home black-and-blue every week, and, finally, he said that I could not get even with Hitler by fighting with people who may have uttered an insensitive or stupid remark. He had great influence on me.

Little by little, I calmed down. As positive experiences replaced the raw memories of horror, I came to trust others more. When I realized that I didn't need to be so self-protective, that nobody would hurt me here, then my naturally extroverted personality reasserted itself. I started talking again, I regained my sense of humor, I made friends, and I did my best to keep up with my fellow students in driving our teachers crazy.

Me at 15

We were a bright group, but we were frisky. For example, Yehuda Marlow was in my class. He ultimately became an important rabbi and judge, but back then he was a handful, like me. One of my quirks was having my scalp massaged. I paid him a nickel to sit behind me and rub my head. My study partner (*chavrusa*) was Shalom Ber Schneersohn; he became the rabbi of a *shul* in East Flatbush, but back then he was always singing – even in class. The poor teacher didn't know what to do with us.

My other famous classmates were Harold Slansky, Ben Tzion Friedman, and Aaron Schechter, a brilliant boy who became a scientist. He was a year older than me and I looked up to him; later he helped me a lot with my high school and college studies.

In my opinion, he was a genius. In fact, they were all bright guys, and we had fun learning together.

My one complaint about the yeshiva was the food. Thank God, Sima fed me on Shabbos, for that was the only good food I got all week long. Her little daughter Vivian would laugh at me because if anyone had any leftovers on his or her plate, they went my way. I cleaned every dish. No food was ever thrown away in my presence.

During the week, I coped as best I could. Uncle Lou, who lived in Philadelphia,[64] would send Berel and me $5 a month, and we would go at night to Symanski's Bakery at Eastern Parkway and Albany to buy day-old Danishes there. For a nickel we got two Danishes, and for a dime we got a bottle of milk to wash them down with. Now that was a treat!

I am not saying that the yeshiva underfed me. It's just that I was twice as hungry as everybody else; it was as if I was trying to make up for all the years that I didn't eat. At the yeshiva I got plenty of food – maybe it was not the best food, but it was digestible. For breakfast I always got a hard-boiled or a soft-boiled egg (though sometimes the eggs were mixed up in the baskets and you didn't know what kind you were going to eat that morning). I got as many slices of rye bread with peanut butter as I wanted, and a glass of milk. Sometimes also cornflakes. For supper, I got a piece of chicken or a couple of meatballs and hot tea. Sometimes there was not enough food, so we just ate bread with peanut butter, but there was plenty of that.

[64] See note XIII in APPENDIX for additional details.

The yeshiva was always short of money. That is, it didn't have any. The Rebbe Rayatz was trying to establish the yeshiva from scratch, and it was very, very rough going. I was too young to understand it at the time.

Getting By

It seemed that my personal cash-flow was at times better than the yeshiva's. I was always finding small ways of making pocket money. For example, I was very good at *leining* – that is, reading from the Torah scroll (which has no vowel marks) with the proper melodic intonation. And through my relatives in the Bronx, I landed a job *leining* on Shabbos at the Young Israel synagogue in their neighborhood. The people were very nice to me there, and when I got ordained, they even gave me a present – the entire set of the *Mishna Brurah,* which I still have to this day. And they paid me very well; I got $5 for every Shabbos, so that means I made $20 a month which was a lot of money in those days. At that time the subway from Brooklyn to the Bronx cost a nickel, a quart of milk cost a dime, a pack of cigarettes cost twenty cents. So with an income of $20 a month, I was a rich man, a *gvir.*

With my little treasury, I set up an interest-free lending club – a *gemach* – lending out quarters to my fellow yeshiva students. I was taught that interest-free loans are the highest form of charity, so in my small way I felt I was fulfilling an important *mitzvah.* Looking back, it might not have been such a good deed after all, since most of these boys borrowed the money to buy cigarettes, which at the time cost a penny a piece. (We all smoked in those days, I am ashamed to say.) When they went home for Shabbos, they got their allowance from their parents, and they paid me back. I kept a little black book with the debts recorded and the repayment schedules. I still have that book.

I made even more money helping Abe Jacobson, doing maintenance at a kids' camp he owned near Monticello in the Catskills – it was then called Camp Machanaim (later it became Camp Beaver Lake[65]) and 400 Jewish boys and girls descended upon it every summer. That's where Berel met Judy Glick, a lovely blonde who was a counselor and who became his wife, and that's where we both got some building experience putting together bunks and cabins, and that's where we both learned to drive.

Nearby was the famous resort – the Pioneer Country Club. I started working there waiting on tables when I was 17, and I went back every summer for several years because the money was good. At first they said I was too young to be a waiter, but I persisted, and so they said, "Okay, we'll give you a job as a busboy and maybe let you wait on one or two tables." So I agreed, and I quickly showed them what I was made of.

At first they had me wait on old people, the *alte kackers*, for breakfast. Old people tended to be creatures of habit, and they tended to come in early. They were there in the morning as soon as the dining room opened at 7:30, and they were done early. By 10:00, I had served them all, cleaned up after them, and set up my tables for lunch with clean tablecloths and silverware.

Meanwhile, one of the regular waiters had the younger crowd. They tended to sleep late and come into the dining room just

[65] In 1979, when it was no longer owned by Abe Jacobson, I bought Camp Beaver Lake and built a development on its grounds called (not surprisingly) Beaver Lake. For many years, I maintained a home there and continued to spend my vacations there with my family.

before we finished serving breakfast. One day they all blew in together at the last moment – a really big group – and the regular waiter cracked up. He couldn't handle it. He went into the kitchen and said, "I can't do it, I quit."

The headwaiter – his name was Mr. Jack Green – saw that I was all ready for lunch, so he said to me, "Leo [they called me Leo over there], go and serve breakfast to that group." I said, "But that's not my station, Mr. Green." He said, "I know, but you've got to help me out."

So I went over to the latecomers, and I said, "*Chevreh*, you're late. You know that, right? Now, what do you want?" I took the whole order without writing anything down – pickled herring, schmaltz herring, pickled lox, plain lox, cold cereals, hot cereals, coffee, tea, orange juice, prune juice. I brought it out on a tray. All this time the headwaiter was watching me.

While I was giving out their first course, I said, "The grill is closing in the kitchen, so if you want eggs, give me your order now." They specified fried eggs, scrambled eggs, plain omelet, cheese omelet, onion omelet, whatever they wanted. Again, I wrote nothing down and I brought it all out to them.

The head waiter was astonished. "How did you remember all that?" he asked me. I said, "How do you remember a *Gemara*? You remember. If you want to, you remember." After that, I had his respect.

In between breakfast and lunch, the other waiters took a break – maybe they went to swim or to play ball. I stayed behind in the kitchen. During this time, Mr. Green would prepare the various fixings – the cucumber salad, beet salad, the pickled lox and herring, the coleslaw. That was part of his job. I offered to help him because I wanted to learn how to do these things. He mixed the various salads in big barrels – he added vinegar, sugar, lemon juice, spices, and then he sunk his hands into the mess up to his armpits and mixed it up. I followed his example and then I asked, "How do you know when it's right?" He said, "You taste it." I tasted it – Phew! It tasted so awful I spit it out. But he just laughed and told me to continue adjusting the flavor. Finally, I got the hang of it.

He wanted to pay me for the extra work, but I just asked for a better station, so I could make more in tips. So he gave me the best customers, the tycoons. They were demanding; they wanted to be catered to, but they left the best tips. I got very friendly with them. Come next summer they were asking for me, "Is Zisman our waiter? Is Leo here? I want to sit at his table." I remembered all their preferences, and they showed their appreciation with *gelt*. My earnings from the summer kept me going the whole year.

By my third summer, I had a big following. But the other waiters objected that I was waiting on too many tables. Each waiter was supposed to have four tables. I said, "Okay, I'll have four tables, but nobody said what size the four tables are supposed to be." I got big pieces of plywood to extend the tops and, instead of eight at each table, I had twelve, at one table even sixteen. At the largest table I put the younger customers who were not demanding, who just wanted to wolf down the food and run outside to play. With them I could take all kinds of short-cuts; for example, I would put the silverware in glasses – all the forks in one glass, all the knives in another – and I would pass the glasses around: "Here, help yourselves." They didn't mind, because they liked me, and I gave them good service.

As far as the more demanding customers, my style was a bit different. I kept a little book of their preferences from year to year, and when I'd see them the next summer, I'd ask, "Would you be having the cheese omelet with the cottage cheese on the side, Mrs. Stein?" And she'd just about fall down.

Sunday night we served steaks. This was popular fare, and I made sure that we didn't run out before my regular customers were served. But one night my best tipper came in late, and the steaks were all gone. I ran back to the kitchen and ordered my busboy to find me a steak. He looked high and low, but there were none. I knew this would cost me a $10 tip, and I was doing this work for one reason and one reason only – to make money so that I could stay in school. I said to the busboy, "Moshe, go into the place where the dishwasher is and look in the garbage can." He said, "No." I said, "Yes." He said, "You don't mean it, Leo. You don't mean it." I said, "Yes, I do." In the end, I went there myself, rolled up my sleeves, dug into the garbage and pulled out a mostly uneaten steak. I trimmed it, rinsed it off in hot water and gave it to the cook, Mrs. Buxbaum, who adored me and would do anything for me. She reheated it, smothered it with freshly grilled onions and surrounded it with French fries. I brought it out steaming hot, and I served it to him. He said, "Ah, now this is a steak! I've been coming here four or five years, and never had I tasted such a steak." And I said, "Let me tell you, never again will you taste such a steak."

High School

My brother got married at an early age. He met Judy in 1951 at Camp Machanaim, and that was that. They moved into a house in East Flatbush, at 91st and Church Avenue, where I was a frequent visitor, known for my ferocious appetite.

I, myself, remained a bachelor until I was 28. People used to tease me, "How long can you learn in yeshiva?" I would answer that I was a slow learner. But there was more to it than that. I wanted to get a *complete* education. I wanted to go to high school and to college, but how could I when I didn't speak English? In the yeshiva we spoke Hebrew and Yiddish, which didn't exactly help me advance in the American culture – it took me six months just to learn enough words to get by in a grocery store.

Besides this, I was missing the prerequisites to go into high school, because I spent my high-school years in the concentration camps. All I knew was basic math, like addition, subtraction, fractions and multiplication tables – "two times two is four" – I mean, *literally* that is all I knew. By the time we were forced to move to the ghetto I had learned the multiplication table up to ten! I was like a kid entering second grade, but I was in my late teens already.

But to even start learning secular subjects, I had to know English first. So I was trying to learn, but I found it very difficult. English sounded to me like you were speaking with a hot potato in your mouth – the sounds were so strange, and there seemed to be no rules. You had to, basically, memorize the entire language. You couldn't just learn the rules and apply them as in other languages. I mean, how come "enough" is not spelled "enaf"? Or, how come it's "mouse/mice" but not "house/hice"?

It took me about 18 months to memorize English, working at it part-time since I was learning in yeshiva most of the day. My model was another *bochur* named Zalman Posner, who was a little older than me. Zalman was a real English wiz – if you wanted to know how to spell or define a word, you went to him because he always knew it. He walked around with a dictionary and learned vocabulary in his spare time. So I started to do what he did, but he told me, "Leibel, you're not going to learn English from a book. You have to speak English to learn English. If you're going to talk Yiddish all the time, you'll never learn. So you speak English even if they make fun of you. Don't worry, just speak." And that's what I did.

By the time I succeeded, I was 17. At this age most people finish high school, not begin it. But I made a deal. I was always good at making deals, and I guess because I was a cute kid with my red hair, people went along with me. So I made a deal with the principal of the Bedford Yeshiva, where I was plodding in the afternoons through secular subjects that I had only been introduced to for the first time in 1946. I said, "Look, I want to graduate high school so that I can go to college, but I don't have it in me to study for four years. It's ridiculous at my age. I'm too old. What can we do about it?" He said, "If you pass all the exams, I'll give you credit, and I'll give you a diploma." And that's what I did. I started studying like a crazy man for these exams – which were called the Regents – and I finished high school in 2-½ years.

The principal gave me all the books I needed. He said, "Here, this is the math book; you have to know algebra. Here is the geography book; you have to know all the countries of the world. Here is physics; you have to know the laws of nature. Here is

Berel and Judy in their wedding photo

history; you have to know the story of America." And so forth. I was exempt from languages because I already knew Lithuanian, Russian, German, Hebrew and Yiddish. The rest he let me study on my own with the understanding that if I passed the Regents with a score of at least 75 (out of a possible 100), he would give me credit for the course.[66] It was a tremendously beneficial thing for me because I didn't have to sit with all the youngsters in high school for all that long. They were so much younger than me. By then I was 17 going on 18, and they were all 13 going on 14. Can you imagine the psychological trauma of sitting in a classroom with kids who were that much younger, who did not speak English with a thick Yiddish accent, and who were culturally on a different planet? Still, I stuck it out for 2-½ years.

Having gotten a high school diploma, I was ready for college. But about this time – 1949 – I had moved over from the Bedford Yeshiva to the advanced yeshiva which was located at 770 Eastern Parkway.[67] My announcement that I wanted to go to college in the evenings went over like a lead balloon. Officially, the yeshiva didn't allow parallel college studies, but since the Rebbe's son-in-law had studied at the University of Berlin and at the Sorbonne of Paris, I figured a deal could be made. My good friend from the Bedford Yeshiva, Aaron Schechter, went to college, but he didn't challenge the system like I was proposing to do; he just quit and went to the Modern Orthodox institution, Yeshiva University.

I did not want to quit, but I was not above the hard sell. I went to HaRav Yisroel Jacobson,[68] who was the custodian of the

---

[66] See note XIV in APPENDIX for additional details.

[67] See notes XV and XVI in APPENDIX for additional details.

[68] HaRav Yisroel Jacobson was the brother of Abe Jacobson, my cousin Sima's husband.

yeshiva, and I said, "Maybe you can help me work this out, because if they don't let me go to college I'll just leave here. I'll go to the Yeshiva University like Aaron did. I know they'll accept me over there." He said, "No, no. Don't do that. We'll find a solution for you."

I proposed that I go to yeshiva in the morning and college in the evening. He said, "I can't let you do that, because other people will want to do the same thing, and it's against the yeshiva rules." But he made me a counter-proposal. He said, "Look, learn another year at 770 until you get *semicha* [rabbinical ordination]. After that, we'll sit down and discuss it. I'm not saying yes now, but also I'm not saying no. Let's see what happens then. If you still think that you want it, that you need it to make a living, we'll see."

He must have thought that I would change my mind or forget about it. After a while, he sent me to New Haven, Connecticut, to teach in a school there. I think he figured I'd meet a girl, get married and stay on. But I lasted only about a month. It was not for me. At that time, I was very uncomfortable with speaking in front of others, and if I had to speak in public, I used to break out in a sweat. So teaching in front of a class was punishment to me. I endured it for a month; then I ran back to Brooklyn.

So, after that experiment failed, HaRav Jacobson tried another tack. He saw that I was good with my hands, so he proposed that I become a *shochet*, a kosher butcher. I learned how to slaughter chickens. This was a good practical skill to have, because in those days you couldn't buy kosher meat in the grocery as easily as you can today. But you could go to the farmer's market, buy a chicken, slaughter it in accordance with Jewish law and have dinner!

This hands-on learning was really the result of the Rebbe's influence. He was so down to earth, and he wanted every yeshiva *bochur* to have all the necessary skills to live a Jewish life according to Torah law. This meant being able to read (*lein*) the Torah in Hebrew with the proper tonal notes; this meant knowing how to slaughter animals in the kosher manner; this meant knowing how to blow the *shofar* (ram's horn) and how to knot the special fringes (*tzitzis*) on the four-cornered garments, as prescribed by Jewish law. This way, if the yeshiva student was sent somewhere where Jews did not know how to do these things, he could fill a practical role in the community.

When HaRav Jacobson saw I was not dissuaded from going to college by the options he offered me, he tried to entice me with a stellar learning partner, Shalom Marozov, an older chassid who was a Talmudic genius and who generally learned alone. Shalom was such a humble man that he meekly accepted the assignment of minding me. HaRav Jacobson's strategy worked for a while and, looking back, I see that I learned a lot because I had such an incredible *chavrusa*. But I never truly abandoned my goal.

After a time, I noticed that there were students who were studying in the yeshiva only part-time; they studied during the day and went out to do work at night, selling Chabad books and pamphlets. So I repeated my earlier suggestion to HaRav Jacobson: "Let me learn in the yeshiva in the morning and go to college in the evening like they do." He didn't agree officially, but he just closed his eyes, rather than force me to choose. He knew I would choose college, so this was his way of keeping me in the yeshiva as well. And that's how I got around the yeshiva's rules. When you can't go under, go over!

Some years later, when I was getting married and went in to get a blessing from the Rebbe, I found out that he knew of my college education. I had studied mathematics and he had also studied mathematics when he went to university, and he said to me, "Since you are a mathematician, you should figure out a good life for yourself." This made me feel good; I understood that I had not gone against his wishes.

Finally, I got *semicha* in 1958. I got personal ordination from the Rosh Yeshiva, HaRav HaGaon Yisroel Piekarski, and also ordination from the Lubavitch Yeshiva, signed by all the other rabbis who taught there.[69] Though I became a rabbi in name, it was not in my program to start preaching from any pulpit. I was unconventional then, as I am now. I did not become a *fein-schmecker*, I did not put on a *kapota* (the long coat that chassidic rabbis wear), and I did not give up my goal of a college education. In fact, I continued to be my wild self, though a bit more calm and mature, now that I was 28 years old, already dating the girl who would become my wife and working hard to get my degree – despite the odds arrayed against me – at Brooklyn College.

---

[69] See note XVII in APPENDIX for additional details.

HIGHER EDUCATION

I went to Brooklyn College – not because it was a good school (which it was), but because it was the closest geographically to 770, and it was free. In those years, if you maintained a "B" average, you were able to attend college for nothing. All you had to do was pay a small registration fee – something less than $20 – that's all. Even the books you got for free if you didn't mind used books.

I got in easily enough, but then the hard part started.

The hard part was not the studying. I was used to the rigorous schedule of the yeshiva, and I loved to learn. What's more, I had a natural aptitude for mathematics, economics, civil engineering and the like. I excelled in those subjects. But there were other obstacles.

For instance, one of the required subjects was philosophy – I had to learn about Aristotle and the other pagan thinkers. That was bad enough. But then one day, as I was sitting in the back of the classroom with my yarmulke on, minding my own business, the teacher started talking about evolution – how human beings are nothing more than clever monkeys. I raised my hand. He motioned to me, "Yes, Mr. Zisman." I said, "You are out of bounds. You are not teaching what you are supposed to teach. Evolution is not philosophy. What you are trying to do is exert your atheistic influence on these young people here and plant doubt in their minds. But you are not knowledgeable enough. You want to discuss evolution versus creation? We could have a fascinating chat about how Maimonides views this subject, and I would be more than glad to discuss it with you privately. But unless you stop talking about this here and now, I'll continue to protest."

He almost threw me out, but I stood my ground, "I have a right to object to your statements, because they're just your opinions, and they do not have a place in this classroom." I was older than the average student, and I was not afraid of any teacher. He stopped talking about evolution, but he gave me a "D."

Then there was English literature – another required course – where 90% of the grade was based on two essays you had to write. Okay, I spoke good enough English, but I was certainly not ready to be a writer. I didn't know how I would pass.

In those years, in the 1950s, there was one kind of chocolate that was kosher – it was called Barton's.[70] If you were invited somewhere for Shabbos dinner, you brought a box of Barton's chocolates. Now Barton's had a practice of putting in nice inspirational articles in the specially packaged chocolates that they sold around the holidays. And I took one of those articles, copied it over (more or less word-for-word) and handed it in as my essay. The professor, who spoke with a refined British accent, was not Jewish, and I thought there was a good chance that she would not catch on.

Guess what? A week after I handed in my essays, the professor addressed the class. She said, "Ladies and gentlemen, I have been teaching for a number of years, and I must say I am surprised. Here is a fellow who obviously has a foreign accent, who obviously is not a native English speaker, but who writes very well. And I must give him an 'A' because of the quality of his writing. His English is perfectly correct. Though it is not high

---

[70] The owner of Barton's – Stephen Klein – was an Austrian Jew who got out of Europe just before the war with his family's chocolate recipes; he arrived in New York where he opened up a chain of kosher chocolate shops, each called *Salon De Chocolat*.

level of English usage, it is nevertheless perfectly clear. And there is a very nice message as well."

The next time I handed in an essay, I also got an "A." Meanwhile, I prayed that nobody gave her a box of Barton's chocolates. As far as I know, nobody ever did.

The history course – which included American and European history – was a different story. I went in to take the final with a friend, who was going for pre-med. (He became a doctor and now lives in Florida; we still joke about our college days.) For the final, we were supposed to read a big fat textbook of more than 400 pages. I didn't care about history, and I read English slowly, about 15-20 pages an hour. So, I said to my friend, "You know what? Let's tear the book in half. I'll read one half, and you read the other half. You tell me what you read, and I'll tell you what I read. It'll be faster that way." He agreed. I read my half and told him, but he had not done his part. So I did the only thing I knew to do – I answered all the questions that I could, and I wrote a lot. I filled up pages and pages, writing about what I knew. The rest I skipped over. It was not quality but it was quantity. I got a "C."

That's how I breezed through – studying hard most of the time, cutting corners when necessary, but overall having a good time. Only once in my college career do I remember being treated unfairly.

I was a math major – a subject in which I excelled without any tricks – and as part of my required courses I had to take calculus. Easy for me. The teacher was a tenured professor, a spinster, who had her rules. The rules were: "There will be five quizzes, and a final. The quizzes will each count for 10% of your grade averaged out, and the final will count for 50%. If you miss any one test, you will get a zero." She made this announcement the first day of class, and I, sitting in the back of the room, paid scant attention. As it happened, during the fall term, the Jewish holidays fell in the middle of the week, and therefore, as an observant Jew, I was out for Rosh Hashanah and Sukkos. Imagine my shock when I received my grade in the mail – "D." I had excelled at calculus. Every test I took I got an "A." How could this be?

I went to see this professor, and I learned the horrible truth. I had missed two quizzes during the Jewish holidays and, in her system, I got zeroes and therefore barely escaped failing. And this was a subject that I knew backwards and forwards! This was not fair!

I appealed to the chairman of the mathematics department. He called her in, and she explained her system. I argued that a Torah-observant Jew could not be in class on the holidays. She said that she did not care; she had her rules, which she had announced at the start of class, and I should have withdrawn from her class. But I could not withdraw – as a math major, I had to take calculus, though she was right that I did not pay attention to her announcement, which was ridiculous as far as I was concerned.

I told the chairman that in the United States of America, there is an exception to every rule, and certainly there had to be an exception to the ridiculous rule this professor had made – which ignored the student's proficiency and merely rewarded attendance. She argued that rules are rules, and she could not bend them to accommodate every student's religion. This, of course, was nonsense because Brooklyn College was closed for Christmas. So I said, "This is anti-Semitism. I am going to inform Rabbi Meir

Kahane [the strident proponent of Jewish rights] of what is going on here. And I will not be responsible for the coverage that will result from the newspapers and television."

The chairman said, "Cool it, cool it. We can solve this problem." The professor said, "I am willing to offer a make-up exam." I said, "You must be kidding. I wasn't born yesterday, and I don't trust you one bit. You *want* to fail me. But I am willing to take a make-up exam as long as the department head administers it and grades it." They all agreed.

"When should the make-up exam be scheduled?" they asked. I said, "How about now." I knew the material. I was a mathematician (even if I was not an English scholar). I had no fears. So they pulled out an old final exam from the archives and let me take it on the spot. And I got an "A." I was told this was the only time in the history of Brooklyn College that a grade which was already recorded was changed.

By 1959, I had finished all the credits I needed to graduate from Brooklyn College. I took more courses to make it possible for me to become an actuary in New York State. After that, I continued on to City College, where I took courses in architecture – drafting, mechanical drawing, and the like. I remember for my exam, I had to design a shopping center, and the grade depended on originality. I did that, and I got an "A." And after the course was finished the teacher even asked if he could buy the design from me. He said I had a very ingenious way of managing the traffic flow, and he paid me $200 for it. He probably resold it for $500, but I was glad to get the money anyway – that was a lot of money to me.

My graduation photo

Besides architecture, I also took courses to become a civil engineer. But I did not a get a degree in either, because I got a job as an actuary, a job in which I could put to use my best skill – mathematics. And I also became a mathematics professor – at City College, no less.

Professor of Mathematics

My road to becoming a college professor was somewhat circuitous because, as I said, at first I put my math skills to use by working as an actuary for a small pension-planning company.

I had originally set my sights higher – I wanted to get a job at one of the large insurance companies in downtown Manhattan – but I did not get a job at any of them. Though these big insurance companies hired many junior actuaries, they would not hire me because my name was Zisman, because I wore a yarmulke, and because I had a heavy Yiddish accent. At first I was hurt by it – how could it be? Anti-Semitism here in America? But that's how it was in those days.

That was my first encounter with anti-Semitism since Europe. It was the same for blacks, by-the-way. Jews and blacks had the same problem finding jobs in the 1950s and early 1960s. Of course, nobody said anything explicitly, but it was understood. And it is part of American history. If you want to take a look at the statistics as to who was hired by the big New York insurance companies of that time, you will find a near total absence of Jews or blacks.

Since I struck out with the big companies, I looked in the classifieds, and that's how I got a job with Goldstein's Pension Planning Company. There were maybe 15 or 20 people working there. We used to set up retirement plans and mortality tables for different companies, like Benrus and Lightolier and others. We did it all with mechanical calculators, as in those days we didn't have computers.

When I got hired, I told them right away that on Fridays I would have to leave early. At first they did not want to agree; the owner was a Jew, but he was not Torah observant, and keeping Shabbos was not on the company agenda. But I told them, "I'll make up any time during the week. I'll work an hour later each day. If you want, I'll work two hours later." So they relented.

I was bored there. I had an office painted white like a hospital and no window, which gave me cabin fever. My supervisor, Mr. Kent, saw I was unhappy and asked me why. I said, "There's no challenge." So he said, "Okay, I'll give you a challenge. I'll give you a difficult project which will keep you busy for a couple of days."

He gave me the project in the morning, and I started to work. By mid-afternoon I was finished. Again, I didn't know what to do with myself. I was walking up and down the corridor back and forth, back and forth, when I caught his eye. He asked, "What's the problem?" I said, "I finished it." He said, "What? That can't be?" I said, "Well then, I probably did it wrong. If you want you can give me the pink slip because I'm going stir-crazy here." He said, "Let's see what you did."

I brought it in, and he looked it over. He said, "It's good. Everything's right. How did you do it so fast?" I said, "I work." He said, "Don't tell the other guys, because if they find out you can finish a two-day project in half-a-day, they'll get jealous of you and you'll have enemies."

I said, "What do you want me to do now?" He said, "Go downstairs, buy the *New York Times* and read the paper. What can I tell you? You can't go home, but you've done your job. Just make sure to close the door so nobody sees you taking it easy." I said, "That's no good."

He thought about it, and then he gave me some great advice, "You should teach math. You're a natural." I was astonished, "A natural? I speak English with an accent. I can't teach." He said, "For math your accent is not important, and a teaching job would solve your problem because you could teach at night, and you could use the extra time you have here to prepare your classes." I was still not convinced. "But who will hire me?"

He told me to buy a booklet, which cost a quarter, and which listed all the schools of higher education in the greater New York area. I was surprised how many there were – seventy or eighty! And he told me to write to them all, which I did it.

I got 13 positive replies. I had a yes from a Catholic school over here and a private school over there – in the Bronx, on Long Island, in Riverdale, all over the place. And guess what? City College also answered yes. I went for an interview, and I got the job.

I worked as an actuary during the day – at Madison and 60th Street – then took a subway to a Glatt Kosher Deli at 78th and Broadway for a bite of supper, and wound up at City College at Broadway and 137th by 6:30 when classes started. I used to teach two or three courses at night. They paid me $20 an hour. And since I had plenty of time to prepare on my day job, I was the best-prepared – or I should say over-prepared – teacher at City College, partly because I was so nervous a student would ask me a question I couldn't answer. And I ended up teaching there for ten years. (Later, I taught at Brooklyn College as well.)

I quit teaching when they went to open enrollment, and they pressured me to bend the rules. Now I am not above bending the rules in a good cause, but what they asked me to do was too much, and so I had to resign.

In the early years, I loved teaching, and I was a very popular teacher. In every school, word gets around about which professors are hard, which are easy, which are boring, which are good. The word about me was that I was fair, that I was entertaining, and that I was Jewish.

After four years of teaching, when I walked into my class, I would see mostly Jewish faces, and a few Asians who thought I'd be sympathetic to their poor English pronunciation, as my own was pretty atrocious. Anyone who had problems with English ended up in my class. My students were all smart, they did the work, and they were a pleasure to teach. My tests were all objective. There was either a right or wrong answer, and nobody complained about their grades, as out of a class of 22 students, 18 got an "A" and the rest a "B."

Then things changed. In the late 1960s, all New York city colleges – Brooklyn College, City College, Queens College – went to open enrollment. The entrance exam was abolished, and anyone who wanted to had a chance to go to college. This was nice in theory; in practice, though, it didn't work as well.

First of all, classes swelled from 20-25 to 35-40 students. It took me half a semester to get to know the students' names, and they had that many more questions. Questions slowed down the class, but I had to cover the book, and if I stopped to answer too many questions, I fell behind. The worst problem was that the students were not prepared for college-level math. Some of them didn't know basic arithmetic like fractions and division. Forget about algebra. I had no idea how to start teaching them.

As before, my tests were objective – simple and straight-forward. Well, they failed left and right. In one class, more than half the students ended up with an "F." Naturally, they were not happy, because math courses were required, and whoever failed a course had to repeat it. They complained. I said, "Let me tell you how this works. I didn't give you a grade – you gave yourself a grade. What I did was mark the papers like a machine. Then I added all the scores together, and whatever the final score was, that was the grade I gave to you. That's all. Couldn't be more simple or more fair."

Getting no sympathy from me, they complained to the administration. I got called down to the head of the mathematics department. He said, "You are too tough on them. Most of the class got an 'F.'" I said, "These students can't do the work. You should not have admitted them without remedial aid. My tests have not changed over the years. If you don't believe me, you can take out the old tests and compare."

He still wasn't mollified; he wanted me to push these kids – most of whom were minorities – through the system. So I said, "You know what? Consider this conversation my letter of resignation." He said, "No, no." I said, "Yes, yes. I told you I cannot change the marks. I'll take your word for it – I'm not in step with today's policies. But I'm not going to do something which, in my heart and mind, is not right. These students should study and earn their marks, not have the school push them through, so they won't be able to succeed in the competitive society."

And I quit. That was the end of my college teaching history. But by then, I already had my fingers in many other pies.

By 1956 I had a saved up few thousand dollars, so I decided to buy property with it. I talked Berel into doing it with me. At this time he was working cutting and polishing diamonds in business with Abe Jacobson, Sima's husband. So the three of us decided to form a corporation which we called Jaberlee – Ja stood for Jacobson, Ber for Berel, and Lee for Leibel.

Through Jaberlee we acquired five multi-story buildings (with more than 100 apartments) in East Harlem for $150,000. To make the purchase, we needed to put down a minimum of $15,000, as with that on deposit, the bank was willing to give us a first mortgage, and the seller was willing to give us a second mortgage. I put all the money that I had saved up from waiting on tables – which was $5,000 – into the venture. Berel also put in $5,000. And so did Abe. Berel's wife, Judy, did the bookkeeping, and I became the property manager.

At the time I knew as much about managing property as I did about modern dancing, which is to say, I did not have the foggiest idea. To show you how little I knew – I had completely overlooked the fact that if we invested *all* the money we had, there was nothing left over for upkeep. So if something broke, we had no money with which to fix it. And things broke!

Of course, we collected rents. But everything we collected went toward the mortgage payments; we had no cushion whatsoever.

A window broke. I had to call a glazier to put in new glass, but I had no money to pay him. A switch broke, or a light fixture, or a mailbox. What to do? Usually, apartment buildings have a super who is a handyman and who can repair things like that. But we didn't have the money to hire a super – I was it! This is what you call "on-the-job training."

It helped that I had some natural talent in this regard from the time I was a child, as I previously mentioned. Now, I put that talent to use. I became a locksmith, a plumber, an appliance repairman. Berel became an electrician. He had actually learned the principles of electricity as a teenager in Kovno from one of the refugees that roomed with us then, and later put this knowledge to good use in the Kovno Ghetto, rigging various contraptions – like electrified teaspoons for the instant boiling of water. Once he almost got electrocuted while cutting off a dangling piece of electrical wire but, thank God, he survived the mishap and learned from it. Though an amateur, he knew what he was doing when it came to electricity. He still worked in the diamond business, of course, but he'd come over after his regular job to help me.

One time, I remember, we had to fix a window, which was a wooden sash window (the type with weighted chains in the frame that allow the window to move up and down). We went to a glazier, bought a box of glass and brought it to East Harlem on a bus. Now we had to cut the glass to the proper size and insert it. But first we had to take out the broken shards and the old putty that held the glass in place, which we didn't know how to do. Berel was figuring it out, sitting on the fourth-floor window ledge – half his body hanging outside, while his legs dangled inside (not a very comfortable position to be sure) – while I was in the basement cutting the glass.

I heard Berel hollering, "*Zvantzig by fir un zvantzig!*" Okay, good. I measured out 20 by 24 inches, took the glass cutter, scored the glass, and it broke into a hundred pieces. Good thing, we bought a box of glass. I tried again; this one broke into three pieces. I was making progress. Meanwhile, Berel was hanging upstairs, yelling, "What's taking you so long?" I answered, "There are a few complications." But by the third time I succeeded.

In Yiddish there is an expression *rebbe gelt*, which describes the "high price" of experience. I sure was paying it.

The seller of the building, who was holding the second mortgage, expected us to throw in the towel. He thought we were naïve yeshiva boys – our thick Yiddish accents gave us away. But if we failed, he would get to keep our money, foreclose on the buildings, and resell the whole mess to some other unsuspecting victim.

To quicken our failure, he informed the city building inspector that the plumbing in one of the buildings was not installed according to the city building code. Of course, he knew it because he had installed it. The inspector came. Sure enough the pipe was ½ inch, but the code said it was supposed to be ¾ inch. While the inspector was checking the plumbing he looked around and found another 200 code violations!

The seller expected that now we would give up. But if we did that, we would lose our entire investment of $15,000, and that was all the money we had. So we couldn't just drop it.

We told the inspector, "We'll fix everything." I knew a Jewish guy – an old man from Poland – who had a plumbing supply shop nearby. I went to see him and told him about our problem. He said, "Why don't you hire help?" I said, "We don't have the money." He said, "Don't worry. Come back tomorrow, and I'll help you."

The next day I went back, and I brought with me the whole list of the violations that the inspector had found. He said, "I'm going to give you the pipes, the nipples, the elbows with the tees, whatever you need to fix it, and I'm going to recommend a local handiman to be your helper. He is not a plumber but he knows what he is doing. You'll have to pay him $10 a day. If you get stuck, I'll come and I'll show you."

Unbelievable as it may sound, we replaced all the pipes in a multi-story building in about a week. And this was hard work, as we had to thread the pipes by hand, using a hand crank which just about dislocated my elbow. Not only that – we had to be careful not to ruin the teeth of the threader, so we had to oil it constantly, and this made an awful mess and smelled worse. When we finished, we called back the inspector, and he gave us clearance.

After that, we were unstoppable. We tried everything – putting up sheetrock, plastering, painting, tiling. We changed doors, did all sorts of carpentry work, and once we even poured cement to repair a whole sidewalk that was in violation.

The tremendous benefit of this experience was that we learned the construction business, and this gave us an entrée into another way of making good money. But that came later.

Meanwhile, with our newly-acquired confidence in being successful "slumlords," Berel and I found other properties going begging, formed an association of investors, and bought more buildings. I managed them all.

But before that, I got married.

Myrna

As I already said, every summer I waited tables at the Pioneer Country Club. From this – because I put my whole heart and soul into it – I made enough money to sustain me through the rest of the year when I studied in yeshiva during the day and attended Brooklyn College at night.

So there I was – the headwaiter in the Catskills – when on a sunny morning in 1957, Myrna walked in the door; she had come with a girlfriend from college for a week's holiday, but I didn't pay any attention to her at first. It was only when I heard the other waiters saying, "Wow! Look at the girl at your table! What a knockout!" that I took notice. I was so focused on my many goals that I just did not look at girls. But after the others told me, I looked. She was beautiful. I immediately walked up to her and said, "Please give me your phone number. When the summer is over, I'd like to call you." She was a very nice girl, and although she did not want to go out with me – I was *so* out of her league – she would not hurt my feelings, so she gave me her number.

She said later that, to her, I appeared strange. My dress, my manner, my strong Yiddish accent, all conveyed an Old World that was out of sync with her New World. But, of course, I did not know how someone like her would view me.

She had heard that I was the best waiter at the Pioneer Country Club, and so she sat at my table. People told her, "Sit at Leo's table, you'll get the best service." And she did. She was a real looker, and she was used to guys fawning all over her. But I didn't know how this was done, and besides that, even if I knew how, I wouldn't have done it – it just wasn't part of my make-up. So she thought I was insulting her. When she left, she gave me a tip, and she wrote me a note. It said something like this (she and I have a different memory of what it said exactly): "Dear Leo ... although your service was good and I am giving you a tip, you were mean to me and did not treat me nicely ... Myrna."

A lot of people wrote me notes – mostly thank you notes accompanied by big tips – so I just ignored hers like I ignored everyone else's. But a few weeks after the summer was over, I called her. She did not remember me. I said, "Hello Myrna, this is Leo." She said, "Leo who?" I said, "I was your waiter at the Pioneer Country Club." She said, "Okay, now I know who you are." And then I said what came into my mind, "The Broadway show *My Fair Lady* just opened. Would you like to go?"

Now Myrna – as she tells it – did not want to go out with me, but she did want to see *My Fair Lady* which was then the hottest show on Broadway, and the tickets were impossible to get. So she said, "Yes!" And I said, "That's wonderful. When you get the tickets, call me." And I hung up the phone.

I don't know why I did that. It just hit me at the time as the right way to impress a girl like this. To be different. Meanwhile, Myrna, on the other end, broke into hysterics, laughing at my *chutzpah*.

A week or so later, I called her again and invited her out to dinner. When I showed up at her door, her sister looked me over, and she asked Myrna, "*Who* is this?" Clearly, I was not the kind of guy Myrna went out with. Although she had been given a strict Orthodox education through the Bais Yaakov school system, she was modern. She was enrolled at Brooklyn College, and as becomes a beautiful coed, she had lots of young men pursuing her. But me – I was a yeshiva guy from Lita who looked like he came out of another age and time. I was a *greener*, which was a derogatory term that Jews used back then to describe those they considered backward yokels from the Old Country, those who were out of step with American ways. Funny thing – I was proud of being a *greener*, I was proud of not altering myself to blend in.

God bless her, Myrna went out with me despite that, and she fell in love with me, and I fell in love with her. And then her whole family fell in love with me, and the rest is history. Fifty years, three children, ten grandchildren, and two great-grandchildren later, we are still together and going strong.

But, again, I am getting ahead of the story.

We dated for about a year, when Myrna asked me, "So what's the plan?" And I said, "I don't know what you mean?" And she said, "I mean, are we engaged?"

We were married in New York on the 28th of Adar (תשי"ט), which was March 8, 1959. The wedding was at Broadway Central, a catering hall in Lower Manhattan, and then we had one of the *sheva brochos* ("seven blessings") at 770. Now I know it is the custom today that each of the seven post-wedding meals is as fancy as the wedding itself, but it was not like that then. I still remember what we served: a bottle of vodka, some soda pop, rye bread and sliced salami. That was it. How can you go wrong with a bottle of vodka and a salami sandwich?

The next day we left for our honeymoon which we spent at the Waldman Hotel in Miami. It was a kosher hotel, of course, and the price of the room included breakfast and dinner. I was concerned about how we were going to have the rest of the *sheva brochos* as we didn't know anybody there, but I needn't have worried.

Checking out the meal arrangements, I noticed that they started serving breakfast at 7:00 and ended at 11:00. I remember seeing some people – I recognized the faces – that came in early, as soon as it opened, and returned just before it closed. They were hungry again. (How did I know? I was one of them.) Dinner was a similar story. It started at 4:30, because elderly people like to eat early. And this hotel catered to mostly old people.

Myrna and I in our wedding photo

We went down to dinner, and I approached a man with a long, snow-white beard sitting at one table. I explained to him that we were just married and that we needed ten men to say the *sheva brochos* after dinner. He recognized that my Yiddish had a Litvish accent, so he asked me where in Lita I was from. I said, "Kovno." He said, "What's your name?" I said "Leibel Zisman." He looked at me hard. He said "Zisman? Zisman?! Are you related to Feivel Zisman?" I said, "He was my Tatte." He said, "He learned by me in Ponevezh."

Who was I talking to? Who had I just asked to join me in the *sheva brochos* for me and my bride? None other than the Ponevezher Rav, Rabbi Yosef Shlomo Kahaneman, who had survived and who must have been in his 70s at the time.

Right away, he went over to the headwaiter and asked to make an announcement to the entire room. And that's how it happened that we had all the remaining *sheva brochos* with 200 guests at the Waldman Hotel, and I felt my father's spirit hovering around me. (All the more so because Rabbi Kahaneman told me many stories about him that I would never have known otherwise.) And I thanked God for this special experience, as I would thank Him every day of my life for saving me and for blessing me with His boundless goodness.

Home and Family

When we got back to Brooklyn, we moved into a one-bedroom, $55-a-month apartment in Crown Heights, at Carroll and Schenectady, near the Novominsker *shul*. The rabbi of that *shul* was the younger brother of the same Novominsker Rebbe who used to put on my *tefillin* at Birkenau. I went to that *shul* once in a while.

Back then we didn't have much money. Myrna worked part-time as a secretary (because she was still in school) making maybe $50 a week, though she had ambitions of becoming an interior designer, an ambition she eventually fulfilled after a slight detour into motherhood. I was managing the East Harlem buildings during the day and going to school at night. Getting a fancy apartment was out of the question; still, we didn't want to live in a dump. And this place was not far from it. It was very dilapidated; it hadn't been fixed up or even painted for twenty years. So I bought a few gallons of paint and a pizza, and invited my friends over. First we ate, then we changed into our work clothes, took out the brushes and rollers, and we worked through the night. With some effort, after a week of pizza, I had a new apartment.

Besides painting, I put new linoleum on the floor, and I bought a new stove and refrigerator. We couldn't afford to buy much furniture. The only things we owned were two beds and a little dinette set – a kitchen table with two chairs and a few other folding chairs. The living room looked big because there was nothing in it.

I needed a bookcase for my books. I had no place to put them and no money to buy a bookcase. So I bought some wood in a lumberyard, and I built it myself. It had shelves with glass sliding doors and, at the bottom, a cabinet which worked like a desk. That was my first handiwork, and I still have it fifty years later.

We lived in that apartment in Crown Heights for three years. Our first daughter, Leba (named after my mother) was born there on January 1, 1960, nine months after we were married. Then came Karen on November 2, 1962, and Chanie on June 23, 1965. I enjoyed teaching my daughters Torah. I taught them all the *parshiot*, the sections of the Five Books of Moses. I taught them how to count and to resolve complex mathematical problems using not numbers but the numerical equivalents of the Hebrew letters. They loved it.

Of course, Myrna left college to take care of the family. Later, when the kids were a little older, she went to design school and became a successful interior designer as well as getting involved in politics.[71] But early on, I was the sole provider. And it was rough going. People asked me why I didn't apply for German reparations to which I was entitled as a survivor. But both Berel and I made a decision not to take any German money. We did not want it; we were not going to help the Germans wash away their guilt with a few thousand dollars. I felt very strongly about it, and early on in my marriage I told Myrna that never was anything manufactured in Germany going to cross our threshold. Once, without realizing it, she bought a set of dishes manufactured in Germany. When the dishes were delivered and I saw the words "Made in Germany" on the box, I ripped it open and broke those dishes one by one. I had to destroy them. I could not give them away. No one in my home was going to eat off those dishes, and I did not want anyone else to either. It was unreasonable because I had already paid for them, but I could not help it. I have too many horrible images replaying themselves in my mind to ever, ever, ever forgive the German people.

---

[71] Myrna started her political career by becoming a New York State Committeewoman (41st Assembly District, Brooklyn). She co-founded WINPAC, the Women's Pro-Israel National Political Action Committee; she worked for Mayor Ed Koch and for Mayor Rudy Giulliani and for Governor George Pataki, helping them get elected. Since we moved to Long Island, she has been on the Cedarhurst Board of Trustees. I am very proud of my Myrna.

Myrna and I with the girls. From right to left: Leba, Karen and Chanie

Myrna and I with the girls. How quickly they grew…

Once somebody told me that I was being too hard on them – Hitler and his Nazi party were to blame and the rest of the Germans were just following orders as all soldiers must. I went ballistic. "Only following orders?! What kind of excuse is this?!" I demanded. "You can follow an order to kill somebody, shoot an innocent person in cold blood even – but whoever forced you to smash little children's heads against a wall, whoever forced you to make naked Jews dance before their graves, whoever forced you to rip a newborn infant in half in front of its mother?"

This was not following orders. This was a people – thousands of German people, the supposed elite – giving free rein to pure evil inside them. Before the war, the Germans were considered the most sophisticated, culturally-refined nation. They were not savages from the jungle nor barbarians from the Mongolian steppes – they were at the peak of civilization. And yet they sank *below* the level of animals who kill only to eat and who do not engage in gratuitous cruelty and wanton sadism. What happened to their basic humanity? What happened to their morality and intelligence, never mind their sense of compassion?

They had their own children and grandchildren who they supposedly loved. They were not bereft of feeling. Had they no empathy, no sympathy – none? How did they live with themselves after they did these unspeakable things? How could they come home, eat dinner, play with their children, go to sleep at night? I do not understand it. I cannot.

And this is why I have never been able to accept reparations from the German government. I have never, ever bought any German goods. Not a Mercedes, not a Braun, not a Siemens – not a car, not a toaster, not an ashtray. And I have never set foot in Germany after the war. I am not saying that they should not go on with their lives. It is just that I cannot forget, I will not forgive, and for this reason I cannot ever relate to them. Oh yes, people say, "It was only some of them. There were good Germans." Well, these good Germans didn't do enough to stop the bad Germans, did they? History stands as a mute witness against them.

Was it stupid not to take their money when I didn't know where the next month's rent was coming from? I don't think so. Some things cannot be counted in dollars and cents. Besides, I never let my financial hardships get me down because every day of my life was filled with *Hashgacha Pratis* ("Divine Providence"). I always knew that – even in the worst moments – something would pull me through. It was as if my parents were up there interceding for me directly with God.

And using them as a model, I made my home a place where anyone was welcome (which initially meant yeshiva students of the Chabad yeshiva). My brother, who lived near Brookdale Hospital (then called Beth El Hospital), also followed suit, becoming the address where patients' families could get a Shabbos meal. We both wanted to be like our father and mother, welcoming all Jews to our homes, even when we could ill afford it.

Of course, we were frugal; we were always pinching pennies. When all the other families went to the Catskills in the summer months, we stayed behind. I taught my children that if you have, you enjoy it, but if you don't, you tighten your belt. You don't borrow and owe the whole world money like so many people do.

I was never a borrower; I never liked owing, and this was the secret of my later success.

Besides that, I was determined to make it on my own. I never wanted somebody else to give me anything. For example, the Chabad yeshiva used to give every student a new suit for the holidays, but I refused to take it. When I went out with my friends for ice cream, I always insisted on treating. I don't know why but I felt strongly about being my own man, like my father was.

ELZEE

When the kids started coming, we moved to East Flatbush –
to East 92nd Street and Winthrop – a very Jewish neighborhood,
in the 1960s.[72] We moved to that neighborhood thanks to my
brother who had a part-time job there as rabbi of a small
Babroysker synagogue – what is called a *shtiebel.* He received no
salary, but by being the rabbi he was exempt from membership
dues, and he got a free cemetery plot thrown in. Now, one
member of that *shul* was an elderly gentleman – in his 90s as I
remember – who had buried two wives already and was working
on his third, a lady he professed in strong Yiddish to dislike. He
offered to sell me a two-family house he owned nearby, so that
his wife wouldn't get it after he died. The price he set on the
property was very low – about $20,000 – and I got it for a $1,500
down-payment.

I renovated it myself, turning it into a three-family house, so
that my renters paid my mortgage. And it came to me that there
was more money in renovations than I was making managing
property or working as an actuary, so I decided to become a
contractor. By then I thought I knew everything there was to
know about construction, renovation, maintenance. I was what
you'd call a *kol boynik* (a "know-it-all").[73] So I said to myself, "Why
not give it a try?" It seemed like the obvious next step up the
ladder.

I called myself "L.Z. Construction," and I printed up some
flyers – saying that I could fix anything, renovate, add, subtract –
and I distributed them myself throughout Canarsie. I chose
Canarsie because it was close to my home in East Flatbush and

---

[72] See note XVIII in APPENDIX for additional details.

[73] The phrase comes from the Hebrew *kol bo* ("everything in it"); in Israel *kol boynik* used to refer
to a trash can and later became slang for a "know-it-all."

because it was a new, cheaply-built neighborhood, where a lot of owners were making improvements – adding rooms, porches, finishing basements – so it was easy to find work there.

As a result of my flyer, a lady called me who was selling ads in the Yellow Pages, offering me an ad for $50 a month. My response was, "What? If after two months, I don't want it and stop paying, you'll tear up two million phone books?" She said, "Well no, it really costs $600 a year, and you have to sign a contract, but we bill you by the month – $50 a month." So I said that I didn't want it, because I could find no benefit to being in the Yellow Pages, which are in alphabetical order, with a name like Zisman; I'd be the last one anyone saw.

But this lady was smart, and she did not give up easily. A week later she called again, and she said, "I have a way that you can be in a prominent place on the third page under General Construction/Contractors." I was intrigued when she explained that the alphabetical order problem would be solved if I spelled my company name L.Z. phonetically – *Elzee*. Now I could be ahead of the other guys. So I said, "Let's do it."

I filed for a name change with the New York State business office, and they okayed it. I became a corporation – the Elzee Construction Inc. And Elzee became my claim to fame.

At first I had a little car, and later a van, that had the name *Elzee Construction* painted on it, along with my telephone number. (That van was a multi-purpose vehicle. Besides hauling my tools, it also hauled my kids.) I did most of the work myself with one helper; I only sub-contracted out big stuff like new electrical lines or water mains and, when I needed to, I hired a professional carpenter.

Elzee Construction van, which doubled as my family car

When I sub-contracted with these experts, I worked with them as an apprentice. This way I learned from them because I wanted to have a basic knowledge of all the trade crafts. One guy taught me plumbing, another cement mixing, another brick-laying. I particularly remember Sam the Carpenter, who arrived for work in a suit and only then changed into his overalls, and who taught me how to assemble a wall. Instead of trying to align the studs within the required space, he assembled them on the floor, then put-up the whole structure and made the adjustments around it; this system cut down the work-time by about 50%. He said that the main part of the job was in the proper preparation, and everything else was gravy. He taught me many tricks of the trade. Other tricks I learned myself – through trial and error – like how to estimate a job properly.

I remember I once built a back porch for a lady in Canarsie. I estimated the cost of the job, wrote the contract and did the work. But I had made a mistake; I miscalculated somehow and lost money. When I realized my mistake, I said nothing to the lady; I finished the job, because I always finished the job. She was so happy. When she paid me, she said, "Zisman, guess what I did for you? Because you did the work so professionally, exactly the way I wanted it and at such a low price, I called everybody on the block, and I told them about you. Now ten people want you to do the same thing for them!"

I was too embarrassed to tell her that I lost money on her job. So I said, "Oh, I'm sorry, but right now I can't. I just signed a big contract. As soon as I'm finished here I have to go there. If they want to wait a half a year, I'd be more than glad to do it for them, but I cannot do it right now." That's how I got out of it.

Another incident was very interesting. Because I was listed in the Yellow Pages, I got a call, out of the blue, from a Catholic priest. There had been a fire in his church, and it was a big job. I told him I needed a few days to compute the estimate. Then I said to myself, "Leibel, wait a minute – what are you doing? This is a church full of crosses and statues!" I began to wonder if, according to Jewish law which strictly forbids graven images, I could even go inside. I called HaRav Jacobson, and I explained about the Yellow Pages and how I got this call. I said, "I want to know if I'm allowed to do any work there." He said, "Well, maybe you can because your livelihood is involved." I said, "But what would happen if I needed a piece of wood while working at the church? I'd have to bend down to get it. And someone might see me and think a Jew was bowing down to a cross. What then?" HaRav Jacobson said, "I think you are right. Don't do it." I felt relieved.

But now how to get out of it? When he didn't hear from me, the priest called me, "When can you start? I like you. You're a local guy. I'd really want you to do the work." I again asked HaRav Jacobson how to refuse this job and not offend the priest, and he recommended quoting him a high price, so that way he would be rejecting me instead of me rejecting him. I figured out what the job would cost and tripled it. But the priest just said, "Fine. No problem. Whatever it takes." God was testing me. It wasn't easy to turn down that kind of money. But I *could not* do that job – I was a Jew who lived by the Torah and that came ahead of any amount of money.

I said, "Father, listen, there's one problem. Since I saw you and spoke to you, I signed a contract for a big job. I didn't know whether you would say yes or no. I thought maybe it would be too much money for you. Meanwhile, the other one already called me back, and I said I'd do it. It will take about six or seven months until I finish that other job." Well, he couldn't wait that long with his burned-out church, so that's how I got out of it. It was a very touchy situation. I had to be careful that he wouldn't think I didn't want to do the job because he was a Catholic. It was a close call.

Another close call had to do with not working on the Jewish holidays. I was hired to add 5,000 square feet to Nathan's children's store near the Williamsburg Bridge, a job which I sub-contracted to an Italian guy. As it happened, the work started after Passover and continued through Shavuos, which fell in the middle of the week that year. I had to tell the Italian guy that he couldn't work on the Jewish holiday. He was angry, "Why didn't you tell me that before? I would have taken another job, or I would have started this one later. Now I'm in the middle and I'm going to lose three days. You want me to sit at home and drink beer at the height of the summer construction business?!" I had to pacify him with a lot of money, so that he would not work on Shavuos.

I never worked on Yom Tov or Shabbos even if I gave out the job to a sub-contractor who technically, according to Jewish law, could do it because he's on his own time. But I never took that short cut. I learned from my first mistake with the Italian guy, and after that all my contracts said, "On Saturday and Jewish holidays the job will be closed from sundown to sundown." That was part and parcel of my printed contracts.

Golda and Me

Before long, I didn't have to worry about churches or Jewish holidays, because I began renovating synagogues, as my career took a sudden upward swing thanks to Golda Meir.

In 1969, Golda Meir – the strong-willed, straight-talking, gray-bunned grandmother – was elected the first female Prime Minister of Israel,[74] and overnight became the most famous Jewish woman on Planet Earth. President Richard Nixon invited her to visit the US that fall and, as a result, New York Mayor John Lindsay was suddenly handed his own re-election ticket.

It was six weeks before the mayoral elections, and the race was too close to call, with the decisive votes to be cast by New York Jews. This is what the *New York Times* reported, anyway.[75] Seizing the moment, Lindsay decided to invite every Jew he could find

---

[74] Golda Meir, a former schoolteacher from Milwaukee, was only the third woman in the world to hold the post of prime minister. She was jokingly dubbed by David Ben Gurion "the best man in government."

[75] *New York Times,* September 13, 1969: "Jewish Voters Wooed; Lindsay and Procaccino Striving Hard to Win Largest Ethnic Bloc in City."

to dinner, with Golda Meir as the guest of honor. But there was one wrinkle – the date for the event fell in the middle of the Jewish Sukkot festival, when every Jew worth his salt would be eating all his meals inside a *sukkah*.[76] So, Lindsay decided to build a *sukkah* that his guests would never forget. But who could do it according to the strict specifications of Jewish law?

I'll cut to the chase: yours truly.

Thanks to the wonderful machinations of Divine Providence, the guy who acted as liaison between the Jewish population and the city government happened to be Lubavitch. When consulted, he named me as the best person for the job.

The assignment was to build a giant *sukkah* in the garden of the Brooklyn Museum, so that several hundred observant Jews could eat there in comfort. (The other invited guests – a total of 1,300 – would eat in the museum itself, which would be decorated to match.)

I went to work with the unions screaming because I was not union, with other contractors screaming because the job did not go out to bid, and with Lindsay's opponents screaming because he was spending half the city's annual event budget on this one lavish affair.

I calculated how much wood I would need – it came out to three truckloads of lumber.[77] I had never ordered so much lumber in my life, and I did not have lines of credit to buy it. I couldn't get enough wood! But with the election hanging in the balance,

---

[76] A *sukkah* is a makeshift hut built under the open sky, and it celebrates God's protection of the Jews after their Exodus from Egypt.

[77] That included six thousand pieces of bamboo (each 12 feet long), nine hundred 2x4s, one thousand 1x3s, and ninety six 4x8 panels!

City Hall did what was necessary to remove any obstacles. I ended up building the largest *sukkah* ever constructed in the United States of America – it was 48 x 144 feet, had a roof of bamboo and evergreen branches and was decorated with tons (literally) of fruit – apples, oranges, bananas, plus pumpkins, ears of corn and what have you.

I bused in yeshiva students to tie, staple, and glue all this fruit and foliage to the walls, which were of wood paneling completely covered with decorations. This was Myrna's idea (she was going to interior design school at the time) and the effect was spectacular.

Now, so much fruit tends to attract wasps and, lest the dinner be spoiled by their stingers, bowls of honey were strategically placed throughout the *sukkah*. This device worked perfectly – the wasps went for the honey and got stuck in it.

But I had more serious worries than wasps – like the danger of the makeshift electrical wiring starting a fire (for which reason we had fire-engines standing by), and like Arab terrorists sabotaging the event (for which reason we had hordes of police standing by).[78] I also worried if my one and only tuxedo – the one I wore to my wedding ten years prior – would still fit. It did! Well, to be honest, I didn't button it all the way, but I doubt that Golda Meir noticed when I was introduced to her as the architect of the *sukkah*, which she pronounced the most beautiful she had ever seen.

Other people said the same thing, and even though I didn't make much money on the project, it got my name out there –

---

[78] Besides these forces, we had three dozen fire extinguishers strategically positioned throughout the *sukkah*. We were ready for anything.

Golda Meir and Mayor Lindsay (along with other invited guests) in my *sukkah*

and many lucrative jobs (like the synagogue renovations I mentioned) soon followed. So the end result was very good for me (and also for Mayor Lindsay, who won by a landslide).

Uncle Tony

One of the more interesting clients that came my way at the time was probably not attracted by my *sukkah*-building skills. He was an Italian furniture-store owner named, shall we say, "Tony," and he would prove to be somebody who would play a big role later in my life.

Tony had wanted to widen a staircase going down to his basement so he could display more of his wares. It was a simple job, and I finished it in a week's time. Because I had a particular way of doing business I always cleaned up after myself, and in this case – to make the clean-up easier – I covered all the furniture in plastic. This apparently impressed him; it showed him that I was concerned about his property, so when I was finished, I was informed by one of the workers that the boss wanted to see me in his office. I went in the back, and heard one of them saying, "Hey boss, the Jew-boy is here," and I was granted admittance.

Now you have to picture this. Somebody pushed a button, and a big smoked-glass door opened up like in a department store. Inside sat a man behind a huge, semi-circular desk. When he stood up, I saw he was about 6-foot-8 and wore a fancy silk shirt opened to the navel with half of Fort Knox hanging on his neck in gold chains.

He said, "Glad you stopped by … I wanted to meet you because I was impressed with the job you did."

I told him thank you very much, and I turned to leave.

Behind my back, I heard, "I didn't tell you that you could go."

I looked at him.

"Listen," he said, "I want to show my gratitude for the extra trouble you took with my stuff." And with that he pulled out a roll of bills from his pocket and peeled off several one-hundred dollar bills.

I said, "No, no, no. That's just the way I do everything. I work clean. There is no extra charge for this."

He said, "People don't refuse me."

I said, "But ..."

He said, "No buts!" He compelled me to take the money, and he also gave me his card. He said, "I don't like too many people, and not too many people like me. But I like you, and if you ever need help, you call me." He said that when I called I should say that I needed to speak to "Uncle Tony." That apparently was the codeword.

Though it was an interesting experience, I forgot about it until about ten years later. At this time, Berel, Abe and I (and some other investors) had bought three apartment buildings at around 104th and Madison, near Mount Sinai Hospital. Little did we know that this area was controlled by Puerto Rican gangs which wanted the property owners to pay them protection money. When they approached me, I refused, and because I refused, every week there was another instance of vandalism – the boiler was torn out, the wires were cut, the garbage cans overturned. The tenants were complaining to the Housing Authority, refusing to pay rent, and it was one big headache for me.

I went to the police to tell them about the harassment and the vandalism. The police response was, "Mr. Zisman, we cannot get involved in this type of dispute. Nobody got killed. Nobody got hurt. It's not a police matter."

I didn't know what to do. I was at my wits' end. The gangs were getting more brazen by the day and they even threatened my life. This is when I remembered Tony – or should I say "Uncle Tony" – the furniture store owner from way back when. I decided it might not hurt to ask for his help – anyway, I was desperate.

I went to see him. His workers told me he was too busy to see me, but I asked them just to say that I needed to see "Uncle Tony." With that I was immediately taken to his back office. He smiled at me and said, "You must be in some kind of trouble, else you wouldn't be here." I said, "I am." And I told him the whole story. "So you want the problem to go away?" I said, "Yes.

I don't want anybody to get hurt; I just want these hoodlums to leave me alone." He said, "Well, you know that I am not involved in this kind of thing. I have a legitimate business here. But maybe somebody in the family can help you." I was so naïve. I actually asked, "Family?" He said, "You know, the extended family."

So he sent me to a bar in Queens, where I was supposed to say that "Uncle Tony from Canarsie sent me." There I was taken into a back office where another Italian listened to my story and told me that his people had to check out the scope of the problem. I was supposed to return a few days later.

When I returned he said, "This is a small job. The ones bothering you are small-time operators. We'll take care of it. No problem." I thanked him very much, and he said, "Hey Leo!" and he held up five fingers. I got it immediately.

Next time I arrived at the building, the usual riff-raff hanging outside were gone. I went into a near-by market and asked the shopkeeper what was up. He said, "You didn't hear what happened here the other night? It was a small war." And he proceeded to tell me about the toughs that came and beat up the Puerto Ricans.

When I went into the building, the gang leader approached me and said, "Listen, there was a misunderstanding. We meant you no harm. You didn't have to send anyone." I said to him, "I'm just the manager here. I don't know what you are talking about."

That was the end of the story. I never had another problem in that building and even people who were always behind with the rent started paying on time. Word got out that I wasn't somebody to be messed with. But I didn't want to test the waters. People's memories run short. So I told Berel, "Let's sell that building. What do we need this kind of headache for?"

And that's what we did. We turned it over to a real estate broker, and he found us a buyer. This buyer was from overseas and barely spoke English, but we were assured he had the money. So we made a deal to sell these three buildings to him for a small profit.

At the time, his lawyer asked us, "Will you take cash?"
I said, "Of course, we will take cash. We will only take cash. We are not interested in mortgaging the property."
"But will you take cash?"
"Sure. We want this to be a cash sale. No paper."
"No paper. Cash?"
"Yes."

Everything proceeded smoothly until it came time to sign the papers and figure out the final closing costs and adjustments – the percentage of property tax paid by this time of year, insurance, utilities, and the like. When we calculated the exact final amount, we asked the buyer to write a check. He looked at us like we were stupid. He reached under the table and hauled up a suitcase onto the table. When he opened it up, we saw that it was full of bundles of dollars. We stared in disbelief. He had really meant CASH, whereas when we said cash, we meant no loans, no mortgages, no collateral, no paper, but we expected the cash to come in checks – bank checks, personal checks, certified checks. We had not expected a suitcase full of small bills – no hundred dollar bills, mind you, just twenties, tens and fives.

By the time we arrived at this point, it was already early evening. The banks were closed. What could we do – he was offering us legal tender. There was nothing illegal in paying with cash instead of a check. And we had agreed on cash after all, though that's not quite what we thought of as cash, but this certainly was a form of it. So, we started to count. And nobody could arrive at the same amount. The bundles were supposed to be $10,000 each, but some were $5 short or $10 short where others had $100 too much. We were going crazy. And finally after many hours, when it was about midnight, we got it all counted and settled. But now what?

I said, "I'm not taking this money out on the street at this hour." Nobody else was willing either. Our lawyer said, "I don't have a safe in my office big enough for all this." So we ended up staying up all night, staring at all this money until the banks opened. We took a taxi cab to the bank where, of course, it had to be counted again. It was an ordeal.

But it was the best thing that could have happened to us. We didn't lose money on the deal, in fact we made a few dollars, and we were rid of this problematic property. The man who bought it had no more luck with it than we did, and he ended up walking away from it, declaring bankruptcy. In some ways though, I was sorry. Eventually, whoever got this property got rich from it because Mount Sinai Hospital ended up buying it during one of its expansions.

My Brother, My Partner

Meanwhile, my construction business was growing. In fact, after four or five years it got so big that I couldn't handle it by myself anymore. I needed a partner. I had the idea to involve my brother Berel, who was very handy, and we already were partners in real estate management. Not to mention we got along like two peas in a pod, as brothers should.

My only concern was that he made a nice living in diamonds, and I wasn't sure that the business I had in mind would immediately generate enough income to support two families. But, thank God, in those days it was not necessary to have sleepless nights about decisions like this; all you had to do was write the Rebbe and ask him. So when I proposed it to Berel, he said, "You know, it's an idea. Let's ask the Rebbe what he has to say. We'll tell him what we're both doing and ask him if it's a good idea for me to leave my work in the diamond business." We asked the Rebbe and his one-word answer came back – *Hatzlacha* ("May you be successful").

Though I was sure it would go well – after all, the Rebbe's blessing went straight to heaven – I still put aside a sum of money, equal to a year's salary my brother would have earned in the diamond business, in case the whole thing went bust and he had to scramble to support his family. I loved him too much not to take out a little extra insurance. Berel did not know I did that; I just told him, "Whatever you do, don't sell the tools of your trade." But Berel simply trusted the Rebbe and came into the business with me.

At first, we used the walk-in basement of his home as our offices. My sister-in-law was our secretary; she did the bookkeeping and wrote checks and kept the accounts. But after a while I realized that it wasn't a good arrangement, because they lived upstairs and with the offices downstairs, they never had any peace. I looked high and low for a proper place, and I found a garage in Canarsie for sale at $55,000 – it would make the perfect office for a construction business, except that we didn't have that much money to spend.

Again, we asked the Rebbe, because at that time – in the 1970s – $55,000 was quite a lot of money. His answer came in Yiddish, *Vos dorfstu dos?* – "What do you need it for?" Again, he saved us, because that neighborhood in Canarsie experienced "white flight" a few years afterwards, and then garages and warehouses were going begging. Also, all of East Flatbush and Crown Heights changed at that time. So had we bought that garage earlier, we'd have lost a lot of money. The Rebbe had profound insight and wisdom. I didn't understand many times why the Rebbe answered the way he did, but if the Rebbe said it, I did it.

Finally, we found a place that was right for us at Church Avenue and Coney Island Avenue. An old lady who was an artist owned that whole block – which had a candy store and exterminator supplies (candy and roach poison) next door to each other. I couldn't afford to buy it, but I told her that instead of paying rent I would fix up the candy store, which looked like nothing more than a wooden shanty. As it turned out, we had to gut it because everything in the whole building – ceilings, walls, floors, beams – was rotten. There had been fires there, and the roof had so many holes you could see the moon at night – you could make *Kiddush Levanah*[79] there. We had to put in new beams, new walls, floors, inside, outside, plumbing, heating, electric, everything. In exchange, she gave me a 20-year lease with the only condition that we pay the property taxes. It was perfect for us and we stayed there for some 20-odd years. We had a beautiful office with a storage yard where we kept some containers and leftovers from

[79] *Kiddush Levanah* is the blessing on the moon, which is typically recited ten days into the lunar cycle.

different jobs – doors, windows, and things like that; we even had parking places.

But there came a time when the owner sold it. According to the lease, we had the right of first refusal – if she wanted to sell it, she had to offer it to us first. If we refused to buy it from her, then she could shop it around. But she forgot and she sold it to someone else. This meant that we would have to start paying rent.

The matter ended up in court. Before there is a trial, typically the judge makes a settlement suggestion. He said to the old lady's lawyer, "Look, your client violated a basic rule. The lease clearly states that she had to give Mr. Zisman the option of first refusal, and she didn't give it. Why should he pay rent now? Not only this, but your client is selling the whole block here. If Mr. Zisman had been granted his option – as he was entitled to – your client would not be able to sell the entire package. I suggest that your client give Mr. Zisman $50,000 as a settlement to drop his claim. And give him another year in the building rent-free because it's a business, and it has to relocate." And that's what happened.

On the next block, on Church Avenue, there was a hardware store called Kramer's run by a Satmar chassid named Yitzchak Abrams. He said to me, "Leibel, you see that picture framing store over there. He's retiring and wants to sell." I went to talk to the owner, who was from Eastern Europe, and we had instant rapport. I made him a fair offer, which he happily accepted. When we closed the deal and I gave him the check, he brought out a bottle of schnapps and cake. He said, "This is a kosher cake. You see it comes from Shifra." We said *l'chaim*, and it was very pleasant all around.

We moved there, and that's where we stayed. For all the time we have been in business, we've maintained the same address, the same phone number, the same name. We did not change corporations every other day, like changing underwear, the way some people do to avoid creditors. We had a good reputation with suppliers, with sub-contractors, with the bank, with the city. And that's saying something in this business.

Government Work

After Berel became a 50% partner in Elzee Construction, we started taking on bigger jobs. We bid on buildings that belonged to the city and that nobody wanted. There were so many abandoned buildings all over New York City, mostly in neighborhoods that had once been white. The whites left, but the minorities who moved in couldn't afford the upkeep and soon enough the buildings became uninhabitable and were abandoned. This happened in the Bronx, in Williamsburg, all over Brooklyn. You could buy these buildings for a dollar if you were willing to invest the money in renovating them.

The first one we bought – a six-story building at Broadway and Berry in Williamsburg – took some finagling because we didn't have a track record in larger projects, but after that we were off and flying.

This first one was a city job – for the New York Department of Housing Preservation and Development (HPD) – and they had certain criteria, namely that the buyer had to have experience in renovating multi-apartment dwellings. I asked them, "How do I get experience if you don't give me the job?"

They said, "There are fifty apartments in this building that have to be renovated. You have never done a fifty-apartment building before. You are not qualified for a project of this size."

So I countered, "Do you think that I am qualified to renovate one apartment?"

They said, "Yes."

I said, "Ditto times fifty. These apartments are identical. And one you think I can do. So it's ditto times fifty." And that's how I convinced them.

We started working on this project, and we realized that we didn't know what we were in for – in terms of the construction we were fine, but in terms of the challenges of working in a violent neighborhood, we were very naive. It was our custom to pay all our workers in cash at the end of the week. Somebody noticed this, and one Friday when Berel was coming with the money, the local hoodlums robbed him; this was bad enough but they also slashed him with a knife across the face. He had to go to the hospital to get stitched up, and he still has the scar from it after all these years.

So we changed the system of paying our workers – we started paying by check, and we varied the days when we brought the checks in. We also got a German Shepherd to keep at the on-site office. He was a pup when we adopted him from a shelter, but he grew quickly to be huge, probably because he was the best fed dog in the whole town. We called him "Boy" and he was very protective of our space; he'd sink his teeth into anyone that crossed his boundary. But he was wonderful with the kids, and they enjoyed playing with him when I brought him home.

Besides "Boy," I decided I should have a gun for protection. I went to the local police station, where they gave me a hard time about it, so I told them, "I didn't survive Auschwitz to be killed here in America. So I am going to get a gun with or without your permission. I would like to do it legally, so are you going to help me or not?" They gave in. I got the proper license, and I bought a .38 which I strapped to my ankle, a .45 which I put in a shoulder holster and an M-14 assault rifle, just in case. I went to the range, and I learned how to use these guns and to use them well.

Because I carried a gun, on more than one occasion I was able to avert a serious crime that was about to take place before my eyes – once a robbery of a grocery store, another time of a jewelry dealer.

One day, I was just coming to the office in the morning (this was when our office was in Berel's basement) with my cup of coffee and bagel. Unobserved by me, my brother's neighbor who was a jewelry dealer was just then leaving his home for work; he apparently stored his wares at home at night, and he carried them in a little suitcase. The robber must have known this, and he approached the jeweler with a knife, grabbed the suitcase and started to run. The jeweler yelled for help. That's when I came upon the scene and saw the robber running toward me. I didn't do much – I just stuck out my foot and tripped him. He hit the ground. I pulled out my gun and ordered him to stay down. The jeweler started to punch him, so that *the robber* was yelling, "Call the police! Call the police!" I said to him, "No, we are not calling the police. Get out of here, but don't let me catch you within ten blocks of this place again."

South Bronx

Besides renovations, we also did new construction. One such project was in the South Bronx – a four-block development of 100 homes for low-income people who had never owned a home before. All the houses were pre-sold with a $5,000 down payment and a government-guaranteed mortgage. The first builder who had won the bid on the project messed up and walked away from the work, and then a second builder got involved, a big-time New York developer whom I shall not name – I'll call him Wilbur Bush to protect the guilty. But he had bigger fish to fry so he, too, decided he didn't want it.

Meanwhile, these poor people who had invested their life savings were waiting. Time came and went, and all they saw was a hole in the ground and no other sign of progress. They were upset, not only because they sank everything into this dream that was proving a nightmare, but also because many of them had given up their apartments in anticipation of being able to move in, and they were living with relatives or in homeless shelters even. The local church helped them put together a grass-roots organization, and they started shaking some trees.

Bush was looking for somebody on whom he could unload this whole mess, when the lumber yard owner, a Polish Jew, suggested me. He said, "I know the right guy: Zisman. This little red-head takes on everything. He loves a challenge." So Bush passed the job onto me with a warning that I would have to sell myself to the members of the community council first.

I had no idea just how hopping mad these people were at the endless delays, but I found out when the local pastor arranged a meeting so I could present my plan. I went over there and found the church hall packed to the gills with screaming people.

The pastor said, "Ladies and gentlemen, I would like to introduce you to our new contractor." They booed: "Out with him!" and "Just another crook!" They called me "whitey" and all kinds of other names that are not fit to print. Basically, their message was: "Who needs another lying white guy. We've been through this already." I said to the pastor, "Look, tell them that I want to say only three things. That's all. It will take not more than two-and-a-half minutes." He got up and said, "Shhh, quiet, quiet. Mr. Zisman, this builder, would like to make a statement. He promises it will be short!" They yelled, "Boo! Out!"

In a way, I didn't blame them because they had two others guys who promised them homes, and they got nothing. But, finally, after what seemed like 10 or 15 minutes, the pastor managed to get them quieted down somewhat. He said, "Hear what he has to say. If you don't like it, you can boo afterwards. But he says he has a message that you will like."

I got up and I said, "I'm Zisman. I'm a builder. Let me put all the cards on the table. One thing I will not do is fool you or anybody else, and you can check me out because I have a good record. If you think I'm going to tell you a story that you're going to have beautiful homes in six months, forget it. Believe me I won't. It will take a lot longer than that. And I am not going to tell you that I'm a very liberal guy and I understand that you're now living in shelters, and I'm going to save you – that would be a lie. I'm here for one reason only. I'm here because I looked at the plans, and I looked at the job. I took a pencil and paper and worked it out over several nights. I figured out that there is a dollar to be made here. At the end of the line there is a profit for me. Guess what? It is not a crime in this country to make an honest living. So I'll tell you this – if you think I'm here to help you, no way; I'm here because, at the end of the day, I think I can come out with a few dollars. I suggest that you go wherever your religion takes you and pray that I'm successful. And if I'm successful, then you will have the homes that you've been dreaming about for the last two years."

Believe it or not, I got a standing ovation. They yelled, "Here is a guy that doesn't give us BS!" "He tells it the way it is!" "The Jew boy's okay! Let him start."

I did the job; I finished it. These little houses looked like toy soldiers – on the first floor was the kitchen, dining room and living room, on the second two bedrooms and a bathroom; there was also a basement underneath. Each block had something like 25 homes, and all were identical. If they weren't painted a different color, you could easily walk into the wrong house. When the owners moved in, they used to invite me to come in for coffee. They'd say, "Mr. Zisman, oh, it's beautiful what you did for us."

This was a little incident that took place – a *Kiddush Hashem*.[80] They knew I was Jewish, because I was wearing a yarmulke.

The houses are still there. At the time I built them they were worth maybe $80,000 a piece. Today, they are worth about $500,000 because the location has become so desirable. I wonder if any of the current residents know what went into getting their homes built.

---

[80] *Kiddush HaShem* refers to the sanctification of God's name that happens when a Jew behaves in such a way that brings honor to Judaism and the God of Israel.

The Rebbe's Blessings

After this we were able to get a "construction completion bond" which allowed us to do work for the federal government. To get such a bond – granted by an insurance company which basically guaranteed your work – you had to have years of experience, considerable financing base, and a perfect track record of completing jobs to everyone's satisfaction. Otherwise, the government wouldn't accept bids from you. Once we got this bond, we were home free because there were very few contractors who were bonded and doing this kind of work. The big builders didn't bother with government jobs because they wanted to build skyscrapers. The small builders couldn't get bonded. So it worked out well for us, as our only competition was a few Italians and one Irish guy with whom we had a good working relationship.

Some of my handiwork

There was enough work for all of us, because there was no other competition.

Working with the federal government was a dream. They were so anxious for people to renovate these slummy areas that they'd put up 120% of the money. We didn't have to risk any capital at all. If it was a million-dollar job, they would give us $1.2 million. While it lasted, this was very lucrative work.

Because we had the "construction completion bond," we were brought into a huge federal project – involving five buildings in Brooklyn on Washington Avenue – managed by Wilbur Bush (the same guy who got us into the South Bronx deal). Although he was the developer on the project, he needed us as contractors because we were bonded while he wasn't. Without the bond, the federal government wouldn't give him the time of day. So he needed us more than we needed him.

To do this project, Bush took out a construction loan from the AFL-CIO, the union, of several million dollars. When I heard that, I told him up front, "There are a few things over here that you have to keep in mind – I'm not union, and I'm not going to join the union because you're giving me a job. If I have to, I'll walk away from it." He said, "No problem." He was an old-timer with deep pockets; he thought he could run all of Brooklyn.

Part of the job involved renovating a historical landmark – the Mohawk Hotel. This was a famous old hotel, originally built in 1903, and because it was considered a historical landmark, we had to reproduce everything the way it was originally. We had to preserve what was there, and what was not there we had to replicate.

Mohawk Hotel

It was difficult, but if we did the job right, then Bush was going to get a million dollars worth of tax credits from the federal government because of the historic preservation. It was a windfall for him, and so he was very interested that we should complete this job – which was very difficult, very demanding – to exact government specifications.

We started, and it was uphill all the way. We could not find the right marble for the lobby, and we had to send a guy to Italy with a piece of the old marble in his suitcase to find an exact duplicate before we could install it. Meanwhile, the union was giving us a hard time. They were picketing, every day, and when that didn't discourage us, they started vandalizing our work – cutting electrical wires and ripping out cables. It seemed like we couldn't get ahead.

At this time, we had a custom that when we finished a job, we sent the *maiser* ("tithe") to the Rebbe. But this time I suggested we send it in advance instead of waiting till we finished. I said to Berel, "Everything is going wrong here, and we need the Rebbe's blessing for it to work out." He agreed, and that's what we did.

When we brought the money to Binyomin Klein, who was Rebbe's secretary, I said, "Look, the Rebbe may ask why we brought it now. If he asks, please tell him that we have a difficult job, and in America there's a custom to take out insurance. We need insurance; we need a blessing that our job will be successful." Binyomin later told us that when he told the Rebbe what I said, the Rebbe was very amused. "That's a novel idea," he said, "Tell Leibel not to worry, it will go well." And he gave us a *brocha* for success.

Emboldened by the Rebbe's *brocha*, I called HUD (the US Department of Housing and Urban Development) and told them "You know the job on Washington Avenue? I'm stopping the job. I'm closing it down, because they're not only picketing, but they're vandalizing the work. I'm not going to do the electrical work twice, because that's extra money. I'm not doing anything more until you come and make an evaluation and add to my fee for having to redo it. If not, I'm walking away."

The man on the other end of the phone said, "Don't close down the job. We will be there tomorrow." I said, "How will I know?" He said, "We'll find you. Don't worry about it."

The next day four guys came, wearing suits with white shirts and ties. They were very polite. "We're looking for Mr. Zisman, the contractor. Is he here?" My super thought they were trouble, and he called to warn me on the walkie-talkie in case I wanted to run out the back door. Of course, I didn't. They showed me badges and said, "Oh, we understand that you called in a complaint because you were having trouble with union vandalism. Can we see the damage?" When I showed them what was happening, they said, "Okay. Don't close down the job. You won't have any more problems."

They must have called the AFL-CIO and told them to quit. I imagined one of the suits saying something like: "We see that you're destroying property on this job. If you continue, we will be forced to arrest your people. This is a federal government job, and federal law says that anyone who meets federal qualifications can bid and be awarded a contract. He does not have to be union, but he does have to pay prevailing wages. As long as he is complying with that, we cannot force him to join the union. Therefore, we urge you to desist from picketing and from vandalism because we will use all our federal power to stop you."

Whatever they said, it worked. The next day, the pickets disappeared and so did the vandalism.

I later learned that Bush had to pay a penalty to the union of $50,000 for violating his contract with them and hiring me when he knew I was not a union member. Even though it was very little money compared to the sums involved, he was mad about it. He tried to get it from us by saying the windows were no good.

He took us to court over this, and he lost. The judge said, "What do you mean the windows were no good? You paid him. If they were no good, why did you make all these payments? What happened by the twentieth payment? You didn't have to okay the payment if it wasn't good. Today, a year later, you say it's not good? Where were you back then?" Of course, he had not complained sooner because, if he had, the federal government would not have paid up. He wouldn't have gotten *his* money. So he had no choice but to say everything was good until all the money was in.

But the windows were fine; he was just trying to recover the $50,000 fine. So the judge ruled against him. When that happened, we counter-sued him to recover what it cost us to defend ourselves – the lawyers, the expert witnesses, the time we had to take off from work – against his lawsuit which was unfounded and capricious. When the case came before the judge, his lawyer tried to discredit us. She put Berel on the stand and asked him, "Have you ever had any formal education in construction?" She thought Berel would hang his head in embarrassment, but instead he answered, "I don't know what you mean by 'formal.' But I would say I definitely had a 'semi-formal' education in construction." So now a discussion proceeded as what these terms meant, and the judge directed Berel to clarify his answer. He said, "I trained in construction under the tutelage of German engineers of the Mohl Company at the Landsberg concentration camp with the SS pointing a gun at me. Would you call that formal or semi-formal?" The courtroom burst out laughing, the lawyer had no more questions, and we won the case.

Afterwards, Bush said to me, "Don't take it personally, Zisman. I sue everybody. And if I win fifty percent, I am ahead of the game."

The Rebbe's Wisdom

Divine Providence and the Rebbe's wisdom saved me in business more than once, and I firmly believe that because of God's tender care and the Rebbe's sound advice, Berel and I became so successful in construction.

For example, in 1987 – just before the big real estate crash – we bought an apartment in Miami Beach. It was in a condo called Carriage Club South at Collins and 50th Street, an exclusive neighborhood which is now called Millionaire's Lane, and thus we became acquainted with developers in the area.

Nearby sat an empty piece of land, which was then being offered for sale and one of the developers approached me about it. He said, "Why don't we make a joint venture? You will supervise the construction, my partner will take care of the legal aspects, and I'll take care of the financing. We'll have a triangle."

It sounded great, but there was one hitch. Time was of the essence. In order to tie up that property, we had to immediately buy an option on the land, which would give us a chance to raise the necessary millions to actually purchase this parcel.

I said, "Okay, I'm going to give you my share of the option money so we don't lose this chance, but I want to put it on paper right now that whatever the Rebbe says goes. If he likes the deal, I will raise my share of the purchase price. But if he doesn't like this deal, then I'm out, and I expect you to give me back what I put in. That's my condition, and if you accept it, I'll go ahead." They agreed and put it all in writing.

Meanwhile, I got a copy of the construction plans – about 70 pages of them. I took them to New York and showed them to

Binyomin Klein, the Rebbe's secretary. I said, "Binyomin, I need advice on this." With his help, I drew up a summary explaining the project and the estimated costs. And I waited for the Rebbe's answer.

Meanwhile, the Florida developers were calling me every day, "What's happening? Are you in or are you out?" Finally after about two weeks, they were *plotzing*. I came to see Binyomin again, and I said, "Binyomin, I would never bother the Rebbe unnecessarily, but my partners are calling me twice a day." He said, "I'll try to get you an answer today." It was Friday morning, I remember.

Binyomin's job was to bring in the Rebbe's mail. He did so and stood at the door awaiting the Rebbe's instructions regarding replies. As he told me later, the Rebbe took my letter, and he read it again and again. The Rebbe used to read something once, and he had it memorized, so this was unusual.

Then, in the right hand corner, he wrote an answer in Hebrew: *Mah lahem u'pizur ha'nefesh shelahem* – an idiomatic expression meaning, "What do you need this distraction for?"

When Binyomin showed it to me, I said, "What does that mean?" He said, "It doesn't mean go forward." I understood. I called up Florida right away, and I said, "The answer is no. I'm not getting in on this project, but I will fly out Sunday morning first thing. We'll have a meeting, and we'll discuss it."

I went to Florida and told them, "Look, this is what the Rebbe told me. The Rebbe did not say it's a bad business or a good business. He didn't say that the numbers don't make sense. He didn't say that you cannot make a profit. He didn't say anything about you, only that I shouldn't go in. Therefore, I'm out.

According to our previous agreement, please return my money. I wish you all the luck, and I hope you get someone else to substitute for me. But I cannot go against my Rebbe."

So I backed out, and the other two took my lead and backed out also.

That happened in the summer of 1987. In the fall, the real estate market crashed. And then they came running to me, "Why didn't you tell us that this was going to happen?" I said, "How did I know? Did I know that we were going to have a crash? The Rebbe didn't tell me. You saw what the Rebbe said: 'What do you need this distraction for?'" But they thought that I knew about the crash but didn't want to tell them. I said, "I told you what I knew, no more and no less. That's what happened."

As a result, one of these developers, a multi-millionaire who is so rich he has his own jet, became a loyal follower of the Rebbe. He came to trust the Rebbe the way I trusted the Rebbe and his wisdom.

The Rebbe and Chanie

Not only did the Rebbe save my business, he also saved my daughter.

When my youngest daughter Chanie – whom we named after the Rebbe's mother – was about to have her Bas Mitzvah, she wrote to the Rebbe to ask for a *brocha*; she wrote in English, of course, and she told him that she was my daughter and that she was named after his mother. She got back a five page letter from the Rebbe filled with blessings and guidance for life.

Chanie (left) with her sisters Leba (right) and Karen (middle)

Two years later, when she was 14, Chanie was diagnosed with severe curvature of the spine – what is known as scoliosis – and surgery was recommended. We followed the general advice of the Rebbe that before any surgery one should get a second and third opinion, and all the doctors agreed as she had a 57 degree misalignment which required surgical intervention.

Then, we heard about a doctor who had invented a new technique of inserting a metal rod to correct the curvature, which made the recovery much easier; the child didn't have to stay in a body cast for years. It was very hard to get an appointment with this doctor, but we managed. When we came into his office, we showed him Chanie's medical records and the opinions of the other doctors, but this apparently offended his ego. He blew up, "What? Are you shopping around? You have three opinions –

what do you want from me? I don't have the time for this." And he tried to show us the door. Of course, I would not stand for this, and I gave him a piece of my mind. I told him, "When I got out of the camps, I made a vow. Nobody is going to mess with me. Not the least of which is you. This is my child we are talking about, and I would spend any amount of money to get her the best possible medical treatment, which apparently means you." After some further exchange of words, he apologized and agreed to do the operation; he said we had to schedule it with his nurse.

Now, the nurse told us that the only available time for the operation was three months' hence on a Thursday. I said, "That's too late, and it has to be in the beginning of the week." This was because the Rebbe forbade us to have a scheduled non-emergency surgery late in the week, which would make a Jewish doctor violate Shabbos in order to tend to the recovery of the patient. The nurse informed the doctor, who by now thought I was crazy. We did not part on good terms, especially when I told him, "You might know medicine, but you are far from knowing life and human beings."

Going home, Myrna was crying. "What did you do? You started up with the doctor, and now he won't operate on Chanie." I said, "We have to listen to the Rebbe. You don't pick and choose his advice. Either you listen, or you don't listen. That's it."

As soon as we crossed the threshold of our house, we heard the telephone ringing. It was the doctor's nurse who said to Myrna, "Mrs. Zisman, you will never believe what happened. In the seven years that I have been working here, we never had a cancellation, but the moment you left our office, a patient cancelled. The doctor can do Chanie's operation next week on Tuesday."

I immediately wrote to the Rebbe asking for a *brocha*. I got an answer back telling me to give to charity, recite extra Psalms, and to take a picture of the Rebbe Rayatz and affix it under the pillow of the operating table. Of course, I followed these instructions to the letter, except that, in addition to the picture of the Rebbe Rayatz, I also decided to affix a picture of the Rebbe himself. On the day of the operation, I arrived early at the hospital, where I demanded to see the head nurse. I can be very insistent when I need to be, and when I got in to see this woman, I explained to her about the Rebbe and the pictures. I told her how important it was that she attach these in some secure way under the pillow of the operating table, and I offered to pay her handsomely for the service. She refused. "No, no, that's not necessary. I am happy to help you." I said, "Are you sure?" She said, "Don't worry, I am a religious woman. I am Catholic, but I have the greatest respect for your religion."

The Rebbe Rayatz

The Rebbe

The operation took five hours. When the doctor came out, his scrubs drenched in sweat, he said, "The operation went according to the book. It was successful. But she will have a very long period of recuperation." I thanked him profusely, called him the healing messenger of God, and immediately informed the Rebbe of what had happened.

Two weeks later, Chanie walked out of the hospital. As far as I was concerned, this was all thanks to God's great mercy and the power of the Rebbe's blessing to move the heavens.

The Rebbe was an amazing man. He became famous for standing every Sunday all day long – without a single bathroom break or coffee break – and handing out dollars to people. Why did he do it?

There came a time that so many people wanted to see him and get blessings from him that he could not grant them all an audience. So he devised a system of connecting with the public with the dollar-bill give-aways; the dollars were meant to be used for charity, but of course people kept them and gave their own money away instead, which is what he had hoped for in the first place.[81]

Once, an observer, who happened to be a diamond merchant, asked him, "Rebbe, how do you do it? How do you, an elderly man, stand there for seven or eight hours at a stretch handing out dollars? Why don't you take a break – stop the line, have a cup of coffee at least?"

The Rebbe answered with a question, "What do you when a consignment of diamonds comes in?" Of course, the man described the whole procedure involved in counting and sorting and valuing the diamonds. "And do you stop for a cup of coffee?" the Rebbe asked. "Rebbe! You are talking about money. You are talking about hundreds of thousands of dollars. You are talking about diamonds!"

---

[81] At other times, the Rebbe distributed honey cake, *lekach* (before Yom Kippur), *matzah* (before Passover), and at the end of holiday gatherings (*Farbrengens*) he shared *kos shel brocho* (from his wine cup).

The Rebbe said, "To me, every Jew is a diamond."

This was the Chabad philosophy that my father followed and taught me. And that's why I never wavered in my loyalty to the Rebbe.

Receiving a dollar from the Rebbe

IN BUSINESS

Since Berel and I went into the construction business, we have renovated more low-income apartments than any other contractor in New York City, working primarily in Brooklyn but also in the other boroughs. Among the most interesting of these was an abandoned public school in Harlem – a one-square-block historical landmark building, dating back to the late 1800s – which we converted into 70 apartments. When we finished that project, the *New York Times* wrote up an article about it, which was featured on the front page of the Sunday Real Estate section.[81]

Described by the New York Landmarks Conservancy as a "Chateauesque" building, P.S. 157 – on St. Nicholas Avenue between 126th and 127th streets – stood five-stories high, but these five stories were equivalent to nine because of their 16-foot ceilings. I realized this after a few months of going up and down the stairs in that place. I said, "Wait a minute. I'm constantly out of breath. Maybe I should go to the doctor. Then it hit me that I was constantly climbing nine stories." (Of course, we put in an elevator.)

This project was managed by the Harlem Urban Development Corporation, funded by the Ford Foundation. The head of the organization, a fellow named Phillip Morrow, lived not in Harlem but in Brooklyn across the street from the Mohawk Hotel, which was a historical landmark building that we had renovated back in 1984. He saw how beautifully it had turned out, and he said, "Maybe we can entice this contractor to come over to Harlem."

In fact, his organization was desperate for a contractor because every one they had approached had turned them down. They were afraid that if they did not start construction soon, the money

---

[81] *New York Times*, March 7, 1993: "Going to School in Harlem – to Live" by Alan S. Oser.

that the federal government had allocated for this project would get re-allocated someplace else.

There were several good reasons why no contractor wanted to do it. First, it was a difficult project, which called for renovating this old school that had been closed down some 15 years earlier. Naturally, when something stands empty this long, it gets vandalized. So the place was in a shambles, and it had to be gutted, but this was tricky because of its historical landmark status. Many items had to be preserved – like doors and windows – and this was a headache to any contractor who'd just prefer to rip everything out and start over. Second, there was no real money to be made. The only incentive lay in the tax credits, but if you didn't need them to offset business profits (because you had other losses doing that for you), the project held no appeal.

The tax credits were just fine with me, so I said, "I'll do it." And then Harlem Urban Development people started hemming and hawing. They said, "Mr. Zisman, you know this is Harlem, and your color is not really the right color for Harlem. You have to have a black partner." I said, "No problem." They were shocked, they thought I would say no.

So we signed a contract.

The first step was that I had to buy this building from the city. This was easy as the cost was only $50,000 – can you imagine such a low price for an entire city block in Manhattan?! I made out a check for $25,000 and waited for my new partner to do the same. But he said, "Sorry, I have no money." I said, "That's not a partnership. That means I'm going to carry it *all*. I'm already carrying you because you don't know anything about construction, but this is too much. A partner in my book matches me dollar for dollar."

I went to the Harlem Urban Development people and said, "There's no partnership over here. He doesn't have a nickel." They said, "We thought that he would put in his share. We are so sorry. But we cannot help. We are a non-profit organization; we couldn't help him even if we wanted to. Our mandate is only to make sure that empty vandalized buildings in the neighborhood get renovated. So there is nothing we can do." I said, "Okay then, I'm out. Goodbye."

A few days later, they called me. I said, "Don't waste your breath. I am not going to change my mind. I am not going to put in all the money." They said, "We think we've found a solution. We think we can make an exception. The thing is that if we don't build, then we'll lose the federal grant, which would be a shame. Our board agrees that if he is your partner, it's only fair that he has to put in the money, but he doesn't have it, and nobody will lend it to him. So under the circumstances, we will make an exception, and you can do the whole thing without a partner."

I thought that now we could move forward, but no sooner had we gotten that out of the way than new obstacles materialized.

When I took out the construction permit, the Harlem Urban Development people asked me, "Did you test for asbestos?"

I said, "No."

So they told me, "Look, unless you test the building for asbestos, you cannot do the job."

I said, "I'm not in the asbestos business, nor do I want to take any responsibility if something happens. Somebody could sue me for $5 million because their child inhaled asbestos." I took out my briefcase and pulled out the construction permit and ripped it up. I said, "You just lost yourselves a contractor. Find yourselves another contractor. I am not doing that."

They said there was no extra money for asbestos and that I had to do it; it was part of my job.

I said, "As it is, the job is tight. No one else wanted to do it. And now I don't want to do it either."

A week passed, and they found $750,000. They said, "We found the money."

I said, "Great, but I am not doing the asbestos testing or removal."

They said, "Can you monitor?"

I said, "I can monitor."

I had to get three estimates. I called in a guy from New Jersey who was an expert in the asbestos business. He came together with an elderly man who had to be in his late 90s. They both looked around, outside and inside. I noticed that the old man was standing and shaking his head up and down, to and fro. Finally, I asked the younger guy, "Excuse me, but who is this?" He said, "Oh, that's my father. This used to be his business. When we go for a big estimate, he insists on going with me. I figured this way he kills half a day and it's good for him; otherwise, he'll go stir-crazy at home." I said, "But he's shaking his head. Maybe he doesn't feel good." He turned to the old man, "Pa, what is it?" The old man laughed. And he explained that he was marveling at this building where he had worked many years ago when he first started in the asbestos business. Back then they paid him to put *in* this asbestos (because it was an excellent fire-retardant). Now he was here again, and they wanted to pay him to take it out.

When the asbestos removal was in progress, the city engineers came to do an inspection. I said to them, "You know that this is a big waste of time and money."

They said, "What do you mean? Asbestos causes cancer; it has to be removed."

I said, "You don't know what you are talking about. Asbestos imbedded in cement is not going to kill you. Asbestos kills if the fibers fly in the air. Here is a building where the asbestos is embedded in the cement. It's not something that flies in the air."

But they wouldn't listen to me. Maybe they privately agreed, but publicly no one wanted to take responsibility and later be accused of exposing the innocent residents of New York to deadly particles. So we got the asbestos removed. The city gave its approval, and the construction again went forward – with more big headaches for me.

This historical landmark had a roof with copper designs, but a lot of the roof was rotted out, burned out or just plain missing. I had to take pictures of the original designs and replicate them in the new installation. So I took off a big piece – a 12-foot piece – and I took it to a tinsmith, an old Jewish fellow. His name was Mr. Schwartz, and he lived in the Bronx. He took a look at this sample, and he said "Hmm." I said, "You see this piece? I need about 70 feet of it in copper. It has to be of the same material." He said, "Wow! You know how much money that will cost? At least $10,000."

But he made it, and I put it on. Truth be told, nobody could tell if it was copper or not, because it all was painted black. The city inspector came to take a look. "Well, let's see which is new and which is old." He really couldn't tell the difference, but that didn't stop him from nit-picking. I got angry, and I said to him, "Don't you remember me? Professor Zisman? You were in my math class at Brooklyn College. You got 87% in Permutation Computation. And you expect me to do 100% here?" In the end, he gave me his complete approval.

There were other interesting things about this building. I researched the original records when it was first built and found that it took them ten years to do it. They started in 1890 and finished in 1900. Back then they didn't trust steel frames to hold up the building, so they put in steel *and* masonry. The walls on the first floor were 24 inches thick. On the third floor they thinned down to 16 inches, and by the fifth floor to 8. As time went on, they trusted the steel frames more. But the end result was that this building was built like the Rock of Gibraltar. We still have that building. It's a good building, and we're keeping it.

Harlem School before renovation

Harlem School, now renovated apartment house

Our Biggest Job

If the Harlem school was our most interesting project, our biggest was renovating 300 apartments in ten buildings near Yankee Stadium in the Bronx. There were more than a dozen contractors bidding on this job with the New York City Housing Authority. The bids were closed (that is, secret), but you were entitled to be in the room when they opened them and announced the rankings. Ours was not the lowest bid, not even the second lowest; ours was only the third lowest, and we didn't get it.

It was a disappointment, naturally, because it was a big job – a $30 million job – and because, in order to bid, we had spent something like $20,000 on the paperwork, which was very complicated. Of course, if we didn't win the bid, we lost that money.

A week later I got a call from the Housing Authority. They said, "Congratulations, you've been awarded the job."

I said, "I think you're making a mistake."

They said, "No. You're Zisman of Elzee Construction, isn't that correct?"

I said, "Yes, but I heard you read out the bids, and I was the third lowest. There were two people before me."

They said, "Well, the guy who had the lowest bid was not qualified because he has a record of a previous bankruptcy. And the one next in line didn't comply with all the regulations. So you win."

They then explained that besides our price and our experience (which was also important), they liked our proposal very much – how we planned to gut these old buildings and redesign the apartments. Of course, everything would be new (except for the walls and floors) – the plumbing, the electric, the windows, the doors, the kitchens, the bathrooms – all brand new from top to bottom. So we were in.

Having won the bid, we now had to apply for a construction loan. We went to the bank – we always did business with Chase – and we asked for $30 million. After negotiating with us for weeks, they said, "We don't want to take this much risk alone. We want you to bring in another bank to finance some of it."

I got very upset. "What risk?!" I took out my business card, "You see this? Read it. It says Elzee Construction. Elzee Construction has been in business now for thirty years and has never been bankrupt – unlike Chase Manhattan Bank, I might point out. Every contractor that I know has changed his name two or three times to avoid creditors. We have never owed anyone a nickel. We don't owe any suppliers. We don't owe any subcontractors. We've never taken a job that we didn't finish. We have a record with HUD, and on this project the government will pay out like it has done on our other jobs. There is no risk. Either you give us the loan, or we're going across the street to your competitors, because you are jerking us around." I said this and more, while my lawyer was kicking me under the table. He was trying to shut me up, but I took it as encouragement.

At the end of my tirade, I got up and said, "This meeting is finished." I took all my papers and my briefcase and said to my lawyer, "Let's go."

They said, "Where are you going? Don't go."

I said, "I'll tell you what. I'll give you until the end of Tuesday – that's 48 hours. Either I get a commitment, or I'm going elsewhere."

They didn't wait 48 hours. The next day, they called me and said, "We had an emergency meeting, and we decided to give you the loan."

And that loan allowed us to go forward with this project – the biggest that we've ever undertaken.

We started working on these buildings which were in sad shape. Abandoned by their owners years ago, they were seized by the city for non-payment of taxes and then allowed to rot. Roofs with small leaks developed bigger leaks; as time went on, with rain pouring in, the interiors started to fall apart from the constant weather damage. Though the exteriors were brick, the interiors were primarily wood – so you can just imagine what happened. We had to gut them.

Before we had a chance to lift a finger, it snowed. Then the snow melted, and all the heavy water caused the roof of one of the buildings to collapse. The roof falling-in broke through the interior rotten timbers, and when it all got through falling, half the building was gone. The police came and set up their yellow tape all around, and within two days we got notification that we had to take the building down, as it was endangering public safety.

We realized that if we demolished this building, we also demolished our contract with the New York City Housing Authority, as our entire bid and the loans and their interest payments were calculated on so many buildings and so many apartments. So this was a disaster in more ways than one.

I called in an engineer, and he told me the building could be saved; the outer walls were stable but we needed to pin them together with girders. I was prepared to do this, but the city inspector said, "No, you have to knock down the whole thing." I said, "It doesn't have to be knocked down. It collapsed because of you – the city. You owned this building for years and you didn't put a new roof on, and over the years the rainwater caused decay which made it collapse. Guess what? I can save this building."

At first he didn't want to agree, but I wore him down with my arguments. As a result, I managed to save this building.

Just because the city inspectors were the so-called experts didn't mean they knew everything. But it took courage – and sometimes *chutzpah* – to go up against them. There were a lot of humorous episodes that happened, though at the time there was nothing funny about them. Sometimes, I felt like I was always fighting to survive – in the concentration camp to save my life, in business to save my livelihood. But all along, I had Divine Providence looking after me. And not just in my professional life, but also in my personal and family life. That's how it was.

The Downside

In order to renovate a vandalized building in a bad neighborhood, you had to take it on as a life project, so to speak. There was funding available from the city, from the state and from the federal government, but they all wanted you to fix it and then *manage* it, not just be a developer who walks away when he is finished.

The New York Times wrote about how this infusion of funds changed the Grand Concourse in the Bronx, mentioning the work Elzee did there.[83] We had renovated two six-story buildings – numbers 1290 and 1326 – with a total of about 100 apartments and, as required, we became the landlords.

Within a short period of time a tenant sued us, claiming his son had swallowed lead paint. The suit alleged that the boy had been sitting on the window ledge, peeling the paint off and snacking on it. And, as a result, he had gotten lead poisoning, which can cause brain damage.

I wasn't really worried, but every time somebody sues you, whether you are in the wrong or in the right, you have to hire a lawyer. My lawyer was all doom-and-gloom. He said, "Mr.

---

[83] *New York Times*, January 24, 1988: "A New Era is Dawning for the Grand Concourse" by Iver Peterson.

Zisman, lead paint is a very serious claim. Since it's a claim for more than your insurance will cover, you are considered the co-insurer, and you have to pay the difference." I said, "No problem."

In the first stage of any lawsuit, they take down all kinds of affidavits and the lawyers cross-examine the various parties. As we were going through this, I told the lawyer, "Don't worry about it."

He said, "You don't know what you're talking about because you're not a lawyer."

I said, "Don't worry about it." And then I explained to him that this renovation was a federal job under the auspices of the Department of Housing and Urban Development (HUD). "In order to do this job, we had to clean out the entire interior down to the brick. The windows were trashed. All the pipes were cut out. All the sheetrock was removed. The floors were cleared to the beams. Fire escapes had to be blow-torched in case there was lead paint on them. When everything was put in new and we painted it, we had to give HUD a sample of every paint used. The paint company had to submit an affidavit that there was no lead in any of their paint. Then, in order for us to get paid, they had to come and inspect. There were three inspectors that came – there was a HUD inspector, there was a building inspector, there was a city inspector, and then an architect had to sign off on top of that. Everything was done by the book, and therefore I am sure – and I have a stack of papers with four signatures to prove it – that there isn't a speck of lead in that place."

He said, "But the child has lead poisoning."

I said, "That may be so, but he didn't get it in this building."

Meanwhile, they had a doctor who testified that this child had ingested lead and that it had to be from our renovation. Everybody lied because everybody was making money. Their lawyer was already counting the hundreds of thousands of dollars that he thought he was going to get from the insurance company or from me. He didn't care who paid it to him.

When we proved everything that I said, the judge dismissed the case. Not only that, he said to the plaintiffs, "You're lucky that I'm not going to charge you with perjury. You wanted to get money that's not coming to you, either from the insurance company or from the landlord."

In forty years of doing business, this was one of a very few times that we were dragged into court. Thank God, lawsuits against us were rare. Here and there someone sued us, or we sued back. This is what happens in business when you are dealing with such huge projects, so much money, and so many people. Misunderstandings happen, and then nobody wants to back down. So you have to sue.

We finished all our jobs for better or for worse. We made money or we lost money, but we finished our jobs. We didn't owe money to anybody – not to suppliers or subcontractors, plumbers, electricians, air-conditioning people, or, for that matter, vendors like lumberyards. We dealt with three or four lumberyards. There were times we bought hundreds of thousands of dollars a month in materials. We paid for masonry supplies, for plumbing supplies, electrical supplies, and ceramic and vinyl tiles. We paid for everything. Either we paid in full or we settled. We sat down, we talked it out, we shook hands, and we walked away.

In Court

Only twice did we end up in actual court – not just in arbitration – before a real judge. The first case involved an old defunct hospital, a large property with a view of Washington Bridge which we had been hired to convert into an apartment complex.

I looked over the job and quoted a price for constructing 50 apartments in this shell. The owner was a lawyer, so he wrote up a contract which spelled out the fees for labor and materials, and the length of time the job would take – which was approximately 18 months. I pointed out to him that the time the job takes assumes that he pays on time, so that the job doesn't have to be stopped because of non-payment. He said, "Don't worry, I have the money."

Then he asked me, "Can it be done in less time?"

I said, "Sure, but speed costs money."

He said, "How much?"

I said, "For every month that we finish ahead of schedule, we get $100,000 as a bonus."

He said, "Good." Now, because he was a lawyer, he said, "Wait a minute. What happens if it takes you longer than 18 months?"

I said, "Then I have to pay a penalty."

We agreed, and he wrote up an addendum to the contract which was twice as long as the contract itself – this was because the term "finished" had to be defined in detail. We both signed it.

During the work, he changed his mind about converting to rental units; he decided to go condo. This didn't affect my deal any, but the difference for him was that he needed the approval of the State Attorney General, which he received. There were other strings attached in going condo, such as that he had to file something called the "black book," which specified everything that was being sold as part of the condo package.

I finished the job three-and-a-half months early, because I offered incentives to all my sub-contractors. I told the plumbing guy, "Listen, if you really push your men and finish the job early, I'll give you a $5,000 cash bonus." He said, "No problem." I said the same thing to the electrician, to the carpenter, to the air-conditioning guy. They all went for it.

This site wasn't far from Yeshiva University, and come dinner-time, I would take 20 to 40 of the workers to the YU cafeteria, where the chef was my friend from Pioneer Country Club days; he was also a survivor of Auschwitz. There, the workers would fill up on chicken, steak, soup, latkes. I paid for it all. Over there, each meal was at the student price, and you could get a good steak for a few dollars. The workers loved it, especially when I told them, "I'm paying for it. Get whatever you want. Go ahead." Then they worked until 8 or 9 at night. In one day, we put in a day-and-a-half or even more.

Since I finished three-and-a-half months early, the owner had to pay me a $350,000 bonus. He did, but he refused to pay what was left of the base contract, which coincidentally happened to be about the same amount. He claimed that the cabinets were chipped here and there, that the tile was no good, that I did sloppy work.

I said, "I don't understand. The building inspector approved it; he said the work was fine. The architect signed off on the job; he said it was fine, which means he looked at the workmanship. Now you come with this whole list of things you say are not good."

This was very unfair. It had been a big job, and the amount he didn't pay was about 10% of the total. Since he flat-out refused to pay it, I sued.

Now let me say this: Don't go to court! The worst settlement is better than the best trial. The lawyers make all the money because they have to prepare for trial, which they bill at rates of hundreds of dollars per hour. The whole thing is one big aggravation, and it takes your mind away from your family and your work. Whenever possible, don't go to court; whenever possible: settle, settle, settle!

But in this one case, I couldn't settle, so I went to trial. I knew I would win the case because all the sub-contractors and inspectors would come to testify on my behalf that everything was good and right. But my biggest weapon was the "black book."

I found out that when people came into the place to buy condos, they were shown the "black book" which had been filed with the Attorney General. One day, I went into the building pretending I wanted to buy a condo. I looked at the "black book" which claimed that not only was everything good in this place, it was *above average*. I asked if I could have a copy. They said, "Sure." It cost $200 which you got back if you actually bought a condo. As far as I was concerned this book was priceless.

I took the book and ran to my lawyer. I said, "We won the case."
He said, "How?"
I said, "We won the case. Set a date for trial."
He said, "I'm not ready for trial. I still have a lot of preparation to do."

I said, "Go to court and tell them that we're ready. And I'll tell you why: in his court papers he says that the job is shoddy. But over here, in the papers he filed with the Attorney General, he says it's very good. So he is lying. Either he is lying here in court; or he is lying to the Attorney General. He cannot have it both ways."

My lawyer said, "You're right. We've got him."

Now, generally, before the trial starts both parties have to have a conference in chambers with the judge. This is to decide certain motions and to set the date for trial. When we went in, my lawyer said point blank, "Your honor, this man is a liar except that we do not know where he lied."

His lawyer jumped up, "You're calling my client a liar? Don't you know he's an upstanding citizen, and he's a member of the New York Bar Association?"

My lawyer said, "Your honor, please put on the record that I said he's a low-life liar. It won't take more than two minutes for me to prove it to you."

His lawyer said, "Go ahead and prove it."

There was a big tumult. My lawyer pulled out the "black book," and he said, "Here's he says everything is good and even above average; it's signed by him and notarized. Here, in the court papers, which are also signed by him and notarized, he says everything is not good. Is he lying here or there?"

The lawyer asked for a recess.

But the judge said, "Well, make up your mind. Otherwise, I'm going to hand down the verdict."

He and his lawyer went into a huddle and then said, "We agree to pay what we owe."

My lawyer said, "No, no, no. What do you have to say about

these two things? Where did you lie? I have to know. If you lied to the Attorney General, then you have to re-file your entire 'black book' because it's no good. And if you lied over there, then you lost the case. If you're withdrawing the case then you have to pay all the legal fees."

The judge said, "Within one month, I want you to pay Mr. Zisman here the full amount of money that you owe him plus legal fees. If not, I'll assign penalties."

All this is part of the public record. He paid. It was the first time that I took a matter all the way to court. The second time, I challenged the City of New York.

Suing New York City

This case involved the Day Care Center of Crown Heights at 420 Lefferts Avenue. Berel and I had bought this lot and built the day care center ourselves, complete with Lilliputian sinks and toilets and two kosher kitchens (one for meat, one for dairy). Some 500 tots attended this day care center, operated by the City of New York, which rented this property from us.

In 1976, the City of New York declared itself broke and stopped paying rent. After we (and every other day care center owner) had received no money from the city for two years, we decided to go to court. People advised us against it. They said that you could not win against the city, and in any case, you could not squeeze blood from a stone. They said that some other day care center owners were able to get a little money from the city after they reduced their rents. But we did not see where that was fair or right. Clearly, the city had money – City Hall was still humming. They were just deciding who they paid and who they did not pay, and small operators like us were the ones they ignored. We could not afford to keep the day care center open without getting rent – as we had to pay the mortgage and utility bills – but how could we close the door and strand all these poor little kids?

We decided to get justice.

Our real estate lawyer said that he was not equipped to take on the City of New York, but he recommended a colleague. I went to see this guy, and I was shocked. He was an old man, in his late 80s, and the suit he was wearing had clearly not been bought in the last decade. The office looked like it had been last decorated in 1920, there were papers piled everywhere with hardly room to sit down. I was seriously worried that this man did not have the wherewithal to win a traffic-ticket case, never mind anything this big, but I remembered that my real estate lawyer said he got results, so I decided to trust his judgment.

The lawyer began to ask me questions, and he was so hard on me and so aggressive, I almost walked out. Finally, I said to him, "You are supposed to be on my side, but you are acting like you are my enemy!" He said, "My questioning is not half as bad as what the city's attorneys will do to you on the stand. They will tear you apart, and I just have to make sure you can take it." I guess I passed the test because we went to court.

Walking in there, I felt like David standing up against Goliath. On my side sat my brother and my old lawyer. On the other side, there were a dozen people – attorneys, their assistants, their stenographers – and they had brought in boxes of books, records, I don't know what all. I said to my lawyer, "Do we need back-up here?"

But he said, "No, no, don't worry."

Finally, the judge walked in. My lawyer stood up and said, "Your Honor, I had open heart surgery recently, and I don't feel so good. Would it be okay if we postponed this matter until tomorrow?"

Immediately, the city attorney objected. "Your Honor, we have here ten people who work for the City of New York, who have made the effort to be present. This matter has been on your docket for months. We strenuously object to any postponement."

The judge said, "Sonny, you may have a degree in law, but you have a lot to learn about humanity. We are not talking about murder here. This is about money. The man says he doesn't feel well, and I see no reason to force him to work right now. Postponement granted."

That's how it started for the city, and it went downhill from there. In his final verdict, the judge said that a little child could have decided this case. He said, "Just because the city is broke doesn't mean this is a reason why its contractual obligations should be cancelled. If that's how the law worked, anyone in financial straits could walk into court, make the same case and walk out having to pay no one. That would lead to chaos. You – the city – have a lease, and you violated that lease. What should the Zismans do, support the city because you have a problem? They should paint and make repairs when they have not been paid for two years? And if the city has no money to pay them, how come they are still paying you and all these legions with you? Clearly, the city decided you all are a necessity but the welfare of the city's little children is a luxury. That's not justice in my book, and it's not legal either."

The judge reamed out the city and his opinion made the front page of the *New York Law Journal*. And guess what? The city paid us the back rent with interest, plus lawyer's fees. It was a total miracle – truly the workings of Divine Providence. To this day we operate this day care center, and we're proud of it.

Berel and I in a recent photo

A NEW CHAPTER

When I retired from active construction work, I busied myself with the Chabad yeshiva and with a soy snack company that I built up from scratch and then sold at a nice profit. Once that was out of the way, I was all set and free to start on the next chapter of my life.

Some people might think that I should quit while I'm ahead. Some people might think that I should be counting my blessings and sitting out the rest of my days with a smile on my face, or maybe nodding off in my rocking chair with a cup of hot cocoa beside me. But the fact is I sleep very little – only about four hours a night – because I sleep the deep sleep of the innocent. I go out like a light, sleep like a stone and awake refreshed. Some people walk fast, some people eat fast, I sleep fast. I need all the waking hours I can muster because I have things to do. Though I am retired from business now, I still have unfinished business – I still have a mission to fulfill and that is to bear witness to what I have experienced and to preserve the memory of those so brutally murdered. I am trying to do that by telling this story.

For years, I did not tell it, partly because I found it heart-wrenching to relive those moments, and partly because I thought no one really wanted to hear what I had to say. This was confirmed for me the one and only time in my youth when I did try to speak.

In the late 1940s, soon after I came to America, I was invited to give a talk in New Haven, Connecticut, where lived a number of Jews from Lita. Chabad had just opened a center there, and the rabbi heard that I was from Kovno, so he invited me as there was tremendous interest to hear from an eye-witness what really happened, or so he said. I agreed to tell my story, and I went there.

Quite a few people had gathered in a hall to hear me. I spoke in Yiddish, which was the only language I knew and, of course, I got very emotional – I broke down in tears, reliving it all.

And I noticed that while I was spilling my guts, people were chatting among themselves and that others were more interested in the ice cream and the pie than what I had to say. And after that I said, "Never again. Never again will I speak and expose myself to the callousness of people. The world does not care."

In their defense, I can say today that perhaps some of them were second generation and didn't understand Yiddish, or were trying to distance themselves from their immigrant parents, or perhaps I was not a very good speaker then. But, at the time, the impact on me was to withdraw. I did not want to be hurt like this again. And I did not speak about anything having to do with the war for 40 years.

Of course, I told my wife and my children some things, but I never told them any details. If my children got curious about anything specific, they had to ask my brother. But then something happened to change all that.

An acquaintance asked me, "Did you have *tefillin* in Auschwitz?" I was astonished, "How did you know?" He was vague, "I read it in a book." It turned out that the story of how I smuggled the *tefillin* and shared it with others was told by another camp prisoner and recorded in the first volume of the *Encyclopedia Shema Israel*, a work written in Hebrew by the Kaliver Rebbe, Rabbi Menachem Mendel Taub, himself a Holocaust survivor. His source for the story was Rabbi Chaim Toter.

After a great deal of trouble, I located Rabbi Toter's phone number and called. A woman answered the phone, presumably Rebbetzin Toter, and I asked to speak to her husband.

She said, "No."

Thinking, I'd have better luck in Yiddish, I made my request again.

But her answer was the same, "*Nein.*"

I asked her to take a message. "*Nein.*"

So finally I said, "I was the little boy with the *tefillin* who was with him in Auschwitz."

And she started to cry: "But that little boy died."

So I explained to her that I was just moved to another barrack, and I managed to hold onto the *tefillin*. Though her husband's group lost track of me, I did not go to the gas chambers as they assumed. "I'm here and I'm alive. So will you let me speak to your husband now?"

"No," she said, "he passed away a few months ago. But he would have been so happy to know that you lived."

After this, somebody offered to take me to the Kaliver Rebbe, the author of the encyclopedia who was living in Israel. The Rebbe had also believed that I was dead, and when he met me, he started to hug me and kiss me and shower me with blessings, including the blessing, "Blessed is He Who raises the dead."

At about the same time that I learned my story had been printed in the *Encyclopedia Shema Israel*, somebody contacted me from Steven Spielberg's Shoah Visual History Foundation, asking if I would be willing to tell my story on film.

Little did I know that my wife was behind this. For years, Myrna had been trying to get me to tell my story, but I wouldn't budge. When she read that, following the success of his *Schindler's List,*

Spielberg pledged to record the memories of every living Holocaust survivor, she signed up to be one of the volunteer interviewers. She was put through a rigorous training program which most of the volunteers failed, but she made it to the finals. And it was she who suggested to the Spielberg people that my story should be part of their archives.

At home, she pressed me to do it until I agreed. And I am so grateful to her for persevering. In fact, without her, I might not have written this book either and would have missed out on so much that is important in my life now.

When the Spielberg people came to film me, I had all my family there – including my grandchildren – and many of them heard the whole story for the first time in detail and in chronological order. They were all sobbing, and even my daughters said they had no idea of all I had been through. They were riveted by the story, which took two days to film, and felt strongly that I should tell it to a wider audience.

Speaking Up

Remembering how dramatic my story was, my son-in-law, Bruce Koren, who was running a kosher holiday program in the Catskills, asked me to speak to his group at Sukkos time. I agreed. I said, "Okay, give me a shot of vodka … it will loosen me up and I will speak." I started talking at about 10 p.m. and didn't finish till 2:30 a.m, and nobody left. And since then I have started to speak regularly. The more speeches I give, the more invitations I get, so that now I am speaking somewhere several times a month – schools, colleges, yeshivas – even Yale University invited me to speak.

I never speak from notes, and when people ask me how I remember it all, I say that I read if off the teleprompter. And then they say, "I didn't see a teleprompter." And I say, "That's because it's playing in my head." In fact, what's playing in my head is a movie and I am just narrating what I see. That's how I speak. And I am an impassioned speaker because I see it as my sacred duty to move and inspire my audience, and to set the record straight.

A poster for one of my talks

In 1998, I was invited to the US Holocaust Memorial Museum in Washington, DC, for the opening of an exhibit about the Kovno Ghetto, and when I saw what they had done, I got very upset. To give them credit, it was a magnificent display, except that in a huge mural of ghetto scenes, they had portrayed the Lithuanians as drunks having fun. I objected to that vociferously. They were not drunks who did not know what they were doing;

they were murderers who happily participated in the extermination of the Jews by the Germans. By the time I was done making my case, they closed down the exhibit, ripped out that whole mural and redid it with a much more accurate portrayal of Lithuanian complicity.

At that time, my brother, the honored rabbi at this event, spoke on the subject of "How will our grandchildren remember us?" He said that they will remember us in the same way that we remember our grandparents. And that is also part of my mission – that those who perished should be forever remembered, that their memory should forever burn bright.

In 2008, at age 78, I participated for the first time in the "March of the Living" to Auschwitz despite my vow never to go back. One of the participants, Rabbi Yisrael Meir Lau, the former chief rabbi of Israel and himself a child-survivor of Buchenwald, impressed upon me that I would have a chance to pass the torch of memory to some 12,000-15,000 young people from all over the world. This was the 20th anniversary march – 20 years since the March of the Living organization was founded with the aim of bringing young people to the concentration camps to bear witness to what happened, and then to bring them to Israel to celebrate the founding of the Jewish state. So that they would never forget. So that they would make sure it could never happen again. So that they would support Israel as a refuge for the Jews. So far 125,000 people have made the trip, and in retrospect I am proud to have been one of them.

At the time though, I thought I had made a mistake. We arrived in Krakow, a place which meant nothing to me, as I had never been there before. Then, we were taken by buses to Auschwitz.

Myrna and I at the gate to Auschwitz with March of the Living

Now, as I said earlier, Auschwitz was a big place with many sub-camps, most of which were labor camps; only the Birkenau section was the death camp where I had spent six miserable months. But at this stage of the program, the participants in the March of the Living were brought to the main camp museum. The buildings there were brick (not wooden as in *Tziganer Lager*, my former home) and they had been fixed up, painted, sanitized. In fact, the museum was as elegant as any art museum could be – it contained lots of photographs of what had been, of course, but to my mind they communicated none of the horror that I had experienced.

I said to Myrna, "I have to get out of there. I can't take it."

I went outside and as luck would have it a mini-bus came by, transporting a few people who couldn't make the march to the end of the line – to Birkenau. I got on and arrived there about an hour before the crowd.

As we approached, the remains of what had once been there brought into focus the picture in my mind. There were the train tracks that ended at the gas chambers (long since demolished), and there were the remains of the barracks, their wooden structures gone, only the brick chimneys standing like a forest of grave markers. In the distance, I saw a few barracks still intact, and I started trudging through the tall weeds to get there.

Yes, this place was exactly as I had remembered it, even though now it stood empty, and there were no Nazis terrorizing prisoners. I reached the barrack door and found it barred by a two-by-four. A piece of wood and a few nails weren't going to stop me – I had come too far for that. Myrna tried to dissuade me, but I didn't listen. I pulled away the wood by brute force and walked in. No one had set foot there in a very long time, and everything looked broken down and dusty. I started to tell Myrna

Interior of Birkenau barracks today

Ruins of Birkenau barracks

Wooden barracks at Birkenau today

how we slept on the three-decker bunks, 30 to 40 of us on each platform, and it all came flooding back with an unbelievable force. I started to sob like my heart would break. Myrna sobbed with me.

And then we walked out into the fresh air.

During the subsequent ceremony, I calmed down. I said *Kaddish* – the prayer of praise to God that Jews say for the dead – and later I gave a talk to the kids that had come from all over the world. I told them what I had experienced, and I told them to never forget.

Since then, I have also made the trip with Birthright – an organization whose mission is to connect every young Jewish adult with his or her heritage. I went with them to Auschwitz, and I went with them to Israel. The trip was filmed, and since then the documentary that resulted – *The Lion of Judah* – has been released in theaters and won a number of awards including the first prize at the Los Angeles Film Festival and the New York

Saying *Kaddish* at the death camps

Film Festival. The film got my name out there and many invitations to speak have followed.

When I speak to these young men and women who don't have the foggiest idea what it means to be Jewish, I become very emotional. And it's hard on me. But I feel I must. I feel I must do my part to prevent the assimilation of my people. So that these youngsters, who have no Jewish education and a weak Jewish identity, don't end up inadvertently doing what Hitler tried to do – eliminating the Jewish soul from this world. But this is exactly what they do when they intermarry and abandon their holy heritage.

I am amazed how positively and warmly they respond to my message. Some even pledge to me that they will only marry Jews, and others ask about putting on *tefillin*, being inspired by the lengths I went to hold onto my *tefillin* in Birkenau.

Myrna usually goes with me, and she is an inspiration in her own right.

Recently Myrna and I celebrated our 50th wedding anniversary, and we treated ourselves to a kosher cruise on the Caribbean Sea, accompanied by our nearest and dearest. It was a time of sharing, laughing, telling stories. As I looked around at my family I could not help but think how differently it could have turned out. Yet God had a plan for me, and in the darkest moments I could never have imagined that my best revenge against the evil that had been perpetrated against me would be these beautiful, smiling children who bring so much goodness into the world.

So every day I thank God for all that He has done for me – for giving me such an amazing father and mother, for bringing me

Myrna and I married 50 years!

up in such a special home and community, for allowing me to survive the horrors of the Holocaust, for reuniting me with my holy brother, for bestowing upon me the wise guidance of the Rebbe, for health and wealth, and most of all for my wonderful, wise wife and my beautiful children and grandchildren and great-grandchildren.

> *Give thanks to God for He is good,*
> *For His kindness endures forever.*[84]

---

[84] Psalms 136:1.

My grandchildren, their spouses, and my great-grandchildren: (left to right, top row) Daniel Portal, Dena Shemesh and baby Sarah, Gabi Orner (husband of Mindy), Raina Koren (wife of Yonaton), Ben-Zion Portal, Rachel and her husband Shragi Portal; (middle row) Max Shemesh (Dena's husband), Mindy Orner, Yonaton Koren; (bottom row) Eliana Shemesh (daughter of Dena and Max), Rebecca Alenick, Randi Alenick, Chaim Portal, and Eli Portal

EPILOGUE

Myrna and I were on our way to the Western Wall (the Kotel) in Jerusalem, when we passed a shop that is constantly playing old videos of the Rebbe. I was not paying attention, but Myrna exclaimed: "Leibel, look! It's you!"

I turned around and saw myself on the video just as the Rebbe gave me a piece of honey cake (*lekach*), which he had the custom of handing out to people the day before Yom Kippur (incidentally, my birthday).

Now what were the chances of that happening? Out of the thousands of videos made of the Rebbe, that the very one with me in it should be playing just when I was passing by – in Jerusalem, no less.

As I watched this old video, I saw the Rebbe bless me for a good and successful year and say to me, *Gmar Chatimah Tova* – "It should end well for you."[85]

And I believed that, with God's help, it would.

---

[85] Literally, "the final sealing should be good for you."

APPENDIX

Additional Details and Family Notes

In Ponedel with Bubbe Tona. Also in the picture, my mother, my sister Tzivia, and (from right to left) me, my brother Chaim Yisroel and my brother Berel

I

My father's brother, Hirsch Leib (Lou), went to Philadelphia around 1914, where a great-uncle named Mendel (who changed his named from Zisman to Sussman) had immigrated in the late 1800s. He was followed there by the other brother, Yosef (Joe). Two sisters, Musi (Lucy) and Meri (Mary), went to Johannesburg, South Africa. A third sister, Gittel, went to Israel; she lived there till age 92. In fact, all those who left Lita married, had kids and lived to a ripe old age. Most of the others did not survive.

My father's sister Gittel

My father and mother with Bubbe Tona and my father's sister Mary with her husband Jacob Flax

II

In 1923, my father accompanied the Ponevezher Rav, Rabbi Yosef Shlomo Kahaneman, who was the Rosh Yeshiva of the Ponevezh Yeshiva, to the World Congress of Agudas Israel in Vienna. It was a long train trip. There were many Jews on board, and my father had the gift of gab – he loved to speak with Jews and to be among Jews – so he was enjoying himself very much. My mother said he talked about that trip for years afterwards. At one of the many stops – and the train would typically stop for 15 minutes at a time – my father got off to stretch his legs and got involved in a discussion with somebody; before he knew it, the train took off without him. Of course, his belongings were on the train with the Ponevezher Rav. The next train was not until the following day, so he had to sleep over at the train station;

come morning, he got onto the earliest train bound for Vienna. No sooner was he aboard than he realized that he needed to pray, but he had no *tefillin*, so he went from compartment to compartment looking for someone who could lend it to him. He found a compartment occupied by two Jews – the older one was still praying, while the younger fellow, who must have finished already, was sitting having a cup of coffee. He said, "Excuse me, can I borrow your *tefillin*?" And he explained what had happened. The man agreed and even invited my father to pray in their compartment. The older man continued to pray, but he gave my father the once over. When my father finished, he said his thanks and left. Apparently the older man was the Sokolover Rebbe – Rabbi Yitzchak Zelig Morgenstern (1866-1940), also known as the fourth Kotzker Rebbe – and the younger man was his secretary (*gabbai*). After he finished his prayers, the Rebbe asked his *gabbai*, "Where did that fellow go?" The *gabbai* said, "I don't know. He left when he finished praying." The Rebbe said, "Go find him and bring him here." So the *gabbai* went on a search through the train until he found my father and brought him back. My father was invited to have coffee and cake with the Rebbe, who asked him a lot of questions. And when they arrived in Vienna, the Rebbe said, "You are a true chassid. Come with me." My father was very flattered, but he said he was sorry, he was obliged to stay with the Ponevezher Rav who was his teacher and who had invited him on the trip.

III
Aunt Bayla, my father's sister, married Yankel Venegrin who served as the unofficial Chabad rabbi in Ponedel because he had spent time learning in Lubavitch, the headquarters of Chabad in

Russia. After being married for ten years, Aunt Bayla and Uncle Yankel had no children, and every doctor they went to told them it was impossible. And then they asked the Rebbe Rayatz to give them a blessing to have a child, and lo and behold, Aunt Bayla got pregnant. I was six years old when she gave birth, which was a sensation, and they had the *bris* ("circumcision") in Kovno. Unfortunately, she, her husband and this miracle child, named Yisroel, all perished in the Holocaust. I later learned that they and all the Jews in Ponedel were taken outside town, shot over an open grave and buried there together.

Extended family. Top row (right to left): my mother, Nosson Venegrin, my father's sister Gittel, Gittel's daughter Basya, and my father's sister Bayla. Middle (right to left): my little brother Chaim Yisroel, my father, Bubbe Tona, and Esther Leah, who married Bubbe Tona's brother, my uncle Yankel Venegrin, and his miracle child Yisroel. Bottom (right to left): my brother Berel, my sister Tzivia and me.

IV

My grandparents on my mother's side, Menachem Mendel Raskin and his wife Chaya Zilpa (nee Reisman), both came from long-standing Chabad families. They immigrated from Zetzk near Moscow to Kovno in 1904. They had four children: a son (who unfortunately was mentally ill and had to be institutionalized) and three daughters: Tzivia, Rochel Leah and Leba Bluma (my mother). In Kovno, my grandfather established a wholesale commodities business. In the mornings, he learned Torah and his wife, my grandmother, ran the store. In the afternoons, he ran the store and she took care of the house. This was the order of things until my father married into the family. My grandfather was a committed chassid, and he was instrumental in building the large Chabad synagogue in Kovno, which was known as the *Chassidishe Shtiebel,* because chassidim of all stripes prayed there.

V

A figure that made an impression on me as a child was Reb Yekkel Ponedeler. He had been my father's first Hebrew teacher, who had instilled in him the love of God, the love of Torah and the love of every Jew, and I got to know him because in his later years – when he traveled fundraising for Lubavitch causes – he always stopped by our house. Later, in his old age, he moved permanently to Kovno. He used to say that he was serving the *ferte sluzbe* ("the fourth legion") because he had served under four different Chabad Rebbes – the Tzemach Tzedek, the Rebbe Maharash, the Rebbe Rashab, and the Rebbe Rayatz. My father saw him as a model of a simple holy Jew, who began each morning with a dunk in the purifying waters of the *mikveh* followed by many hours of prayer. When the war broke out, Reb Yekkel was 96 years old, and one day he went to the *mikveh* as usual, and then he went home to lie down. When his son-in-law, who was up in years himself, expressed surprise that he did not go to pray, he answered, "Enough." Then he said *Vidui* (the "Confession" prayer before dying), closed his eyes and passed away. He'd had a tremendous impact on my father, perhaps because he had been his first teacher and a kind of father-replacement figure. The many lessons in Torah that my father had learned from Reb Yekkel he tried to pass on to his children, though more of it was absorbed by my brother than by me.

VI

My mother's sister, my Aunt Rochel Leah, married Avrohom Budnov, who worked in my father's store as an outside salesman. They had nine children, but only three of them survived the Holocaust: Shalom Ber, Sarah and Ella. Shalom Ber got married to Luba Horwitz and went to live in Australia. Sarah got married to Leibel Raskin, remained in Russia through the war, ended up in Riga, and came to Israel with her husband and two children in 1969. Ella got married to Aharon Natan Gringrass and also went to live in Israel.

VII

Sima was the only child of my Aunt Tzivia (my mother's sister) and her first husband Avrohom Levin who died at an early age. Avrohom's sister Shaina married HaRav Yisroel Jacobson who was sent to Brooklyn in 1925 to establish a Chabad yeshiva there. It was known that HaRav Jacobson had three younger unmarried brothers and, in 1933, Sima was dispatched to visit her Aunt

Shaina with an eye on making a match with one of them, and sure enough she married the youngest, Avrohom (Abe). Thus Sima became a sister-in-law to HaRav Jacobson, who was a very prominent figure at Chabad headquarters in the US. She had one daughter, Vivian. Sima was most kind to me, but she died before age 50.

My mother (left) with Aunt Shaina (right) and my father's sisters Mary and Bayla in between.

VIII

After my Aunt Tzivia's first husband, Avrohom Levin, passed away, she remarried, and with her second husband Reb Pinchas Mintz (also known as Pinyeh Mintz Azaritzer) she had 12 more children, 11 of whom perished in the Holocaust. Reb Pinchas was trained to perform circumcisions (that is, he was a *mohel*) and he was also a teacher and director of the *cheder* which I attended.

He primarily worked in the Jewish hospital, Bikur Holim, where any poor person could be treated for free. Many a time, he would call my father to officiate at a circumcision, and then my father would pay for the requisite circumcision feast.

IX

During the communist rule of Lithuania, a neighbor of ours, Mr. Charass, was awakened in the middle of the night by the communist police because his son, 14 years old, having received a shining red star in school for being a good communist, informed them that his father hid some of his business assets when the commissars took away his store. The father was taken to prison and the son was proclaimed a hero. That is what the communists taught children to do.

X

When Chiune Sugihara was dispensing Japanese visas to Jews, the Modzitzer Rebbe – Rabbi Shaul Yedidya Elazar Taub (1886-1947) – and his two sons came to stay with us. A tall, imposing man, the Modzitzer Rebbe was famous for his songs, and he organized a *farbrengen* – a joyous fest – at the Alexander Restaurant, the kosher eatery in Kovno, as a way of raising funds for his impending flight to Japan. Eventually, he and some family members reached the US and settled in Brooklyn where the Rebbe rebuilt his sect. He was a gifted songwriter and wrote over 1,000 chassidic melodies.

Another illustrious guest was the Amshinover Rebbe – Rabbi Shimon Sholom Kalish (1882-1954) – who was also looking for a way out for his family and his students. He was a major driving force behind the exodus of thousands of young men from various yeshivas to Shanghai. While he was making these arrangements he stayed in our house for a few months (or so it seemed to me). In contrast to the Modzitzer Rebbe, who was a big happy guy, the Amshinover Rebbe was frail and sad, weeping through his prayers which went on for hours. When he left, my father gave him a *peltz*, a beautiful fur-lined, floor-length coat with a high collar, and also lent him money. After the war, when my brother and I met him in Brooklyn, the Amshinover Rebbe gave us back all the money he borrowed, and he also wanted to give us the coat, but we did not want it. What would we do with a *peltz* in Brooklyn? So he had it appraised, sold it, and he insisted that we take the proceeds.

My brother remembers many other illustrious house guests, but I was only eight and while I knew these were important people, there were so very many of them, my poor little head could not contain all their names. I do know that Rav Moshe Leib Rothstein, the secretary of the Rebbe Rayatz, stayed with us, and also Rav Shmuel Zalmanov, who came from a very prestigious Lubavitcher family and was the editor of the periodical *HaTomim*, which was published in Poland before the war. Both were close friends of my father.

XI

Unlike so many who became despondent in the ghetto, my father always had a positive attitude and found sustenance in *Chassidus*. After praying in synagogues was banned, he organized a *minyan* in our house. He always made a point of having the third meal on Shabbos, when chassidim believe – as the *Zohar*, the chief work of Kabbalah, teaches – that the extra soul which visits each person on Shabbos is getting ready to depart, and this is the time to capture its special wisdom and insights. My brother remembers a chassidic discourse (*ma'amar*) that my father gave at third meal. It was an interpretation of a verse in Psalms 104:23. This verse reads, literally, "Man goes out to work, laboring until the evening (*orev*)," but it is interpreted by *Chassidus* as "Man goes out to work, serving God until it is pleasant (*orev*)." My father explained that when a man is learning a trade, he finds the work difficult until he masters his craft, but then he takes pleasure in his skill. So it is with the service of God in this world. One of the men present disagreed, arguing that the Hebrew for pleasant is *na'im* not *orev*. In response, my father opened the Book of Psalms to 104:34, where a form of the same Hebrew word appears in a different context and the only way it can be understood is: "May my words be pleasant (*y'erav*)…"

XII

The wheelchair-bound Rebbe Rayatz prayed alone in his study, but the door to the next room (where the *minyan* had gathered) was left open. Only when it came time for the Torah reading was the Torah scroll brought to the Rebbe with a few men accompanying it. It was a special privilege to pray with the Rebbe and only the senior chassidim were invited. Occasionally, there was space for one or two more (if one of the regulars was sick) and many waited outside the door hoping for a chance to get in. The future Rebbe would come with a key, which he wore on a specially constructed elastic belt. The key had two holes drilled into it so that the belt could pass through it, and he would stretch the elastic – without removing the belt – to use the key. He'd unlock the door and hold it open, nodding to me to come in. So I prayed with that special *minyan* until the Rebbe Rayatz passed away in 1950.

XIII

My father's brother, Hirsch Leib – known to me as Uncle Lou – was a widower who was not religious. But whenever he came to visit us, he'd always wear a yarmulke, and he'd take us to a kosher restaurant. A few times, he invited us to Philadelphia to meet our other relatives there – all of whom went by the last name Sussman – and he was always very solicitous about our dietary needs. While he was alive, he wrote a family newsletter and organized frequent reunions to keep everyone in touch. I remember that the other brother, Uncle Joe, played the violin by heart, and there was a cousin named Morris who was a professor of ancient and classic languages, with whom Berel argued ferociously about religion. I once made a statement that reading and understanding Maimonides was more challenging than any academic subject, and he challenged me to go to college to see for myself. I took up that challenge and partly because of him went to college to get a degree in mathematics.

XIV

In the late 1940s, Chabad's Bedford Yeshiva had an arrangement with HaRav Yitzchak Hutner (who was very friendly with the Rebbe) of the Chaim Berlin High School, which was an accredited school and which technically granted the diplomas. If I had attended Chaim Berlin, I would have needed to pass the Regents with a score of 65% only. But HaRav Hutner set the bar higher for us Chabadniks because he correctly sensed that, as yeshiva students, we gave short shrift to secular subjects, and he did not want our low scores to reflect poorly on Chaim Berlin's standards.

XV

In the late 1940s, the Chabad Yeshiva for advanced students was located at 770 Eastern Parkway. I remember the Rebbe (who was not yet the Rebbe) had an office on the first floor. He worked as an assistant to his father-in-law; he was always on the move delivering the Rebbe's letters – probably soliciting donations to keep us all afloat – and he was also involved in education. On the side of the building, there was a yard where we used to play ball. The garage, which was in the basement and which took up the entire length of the building, was a place for weddings. The Rebbe's library was also there. Reb Chaim Liberman, who was the librarian, knew every book – where it was and what it was – and that's how things were for many years.

XVI

When I began learning at the 770 Yeshiva, Rav Yisroel Gustman was still the Rosh Yeshiva, but soon after, he vacated that position. He was not a Lubavitcher; he was not even a chassid; he was a *misnagid.* How did he ever become a Rosh Yeshiva of an advanced chassidic yeshiva? Well, for one thing, he was a genius (*gaon*) in *Gemara,* and the Rebbe Rayatz wanted a high standard of scholarship when he set up this yeshiva upon arriving in the U.S. in 1940. During the war years, so many Chabad teachers were trapped in Eastern Europe and most of them never made it out. So Rav Gustman was the best the Rebbe could get. But after the war, problems developed with his approach. Two older Chabad chassidim – Dovid Raskin and Sholom Marozov – came over from Russia, and they followed the pattern that was familiar to them from back home which, in fact, was the Lubavitch way. They studied *Chassidus* in preparation for prayer and prayed afterwards, which meant they prayed late. Rav Gustman would not have this, as it disrupted his schedule. This upset the older chassidim and led to complaints and bad feelings. In 1950, when the Rebbe Rayatz passed away, the Rebbe said, "It's time we should have our own Rosh Yeshiva." And Rabbi Yisroel Piekarski was recruited for the job. He was also not Lubavitch; he was a Gerrer chassid, but at least he had a chassidic background.

XVII

After I got married, I used to continue to attend Rabbi Piekarski's classes. As I was not officially a student in the yeshiva, I sat in the next room where I could still hear him through the open door. I noticed that whenever I walked in, he rose from his chair. At first I thought this was a coincidence, but then I realized he was rising for me. I went to him and said, "HaRav, this embarrasses me. I cannot come up to your ankles in learning. I don't deserve this. If you continue to stand for me, I will stop coming." He said, "Reb Leibel, I am not doing it for you. I am doing it for me, because I am the one who ordained you as a rabbi. If I don't get up for you, it means that my *semicha* is not worth a nickel." He turned the tables right on me. I said, "Okay, okay. I'll continue to come, but please don't make it so obvious."

XVIII

After living a few years in East Flatbush, we moved to Canarsie and then back to Flatbush again. Now we are in Long Island because this is where the kids live. We moved there because my wife said, "You know, all the children are there, the grandchildren are there, and they're starting to grow up; they're teenagers. We hardly know them, and they hardly know us. We see them once a month, if that." So we moved.

Myrna and I with the girls

The house we bought was an old house. But I knocked it down in order to start fresh. I called in bulldozers, and they leveled the old thing to the ground. One day, Myrna passed by and said, "You know, I don't know where the house we bought is. I thought it was number 40. But I see a piece of land there." I said, "I forgot to tell you – I leveled it." I had gone inside and looked it over. I saw there was nothing there to fix; there were no redeeming features to this house. It was not worthwhile saving any of it or renovating. The basement was not even six-feet high. I'm not a tall guy, but I could touch the ceiling with my hand. It was not a basement; it was a cellar. On the first floor nothing was straight; everything was crooked. The doors didn't close, the windows didn't open, and the second floor was just as bad. The bedrooms were small and had no closets. The bathrooms were original with cracked, discolored tiles. The bathtubs were still on legs. I decided to get rid of it all and start fresh. We live in that house now. I hope we won't have to move unless *Moshiach* comes, and we go to Israel. And since I hope that day is soon, I already have an apartment ready in Jerusalem. It's walking distance from the Western Wall (*Kotel*). In the meantime, the children and the grand-children have a place to go when they want to connect with the land.

My daughter Leba (third from right), her husband Bruce Koren (third from left) and family at the wedding of my granddaughter Mindy

My daughter Karen (second from left), her husband David Portal (right) and
family at the wedding of my grandson Shragi

My daughter Chanie, her husband Alan Greif, and my granddaughters Randi
(right) and Rebecca (left)

Myrna and I celebrating our 50th anniversary

Myrna and I celebrating my 80th birthday

ACKNOWLEDGMENTS

First of all, I must thank my brother Berel, who lived this story with me – from beginning to end. He contributed invaluable input, and I relied totally on his memory, especially for recollections of our family's years in Lita. He has always been, and continues to be, a guiding light in my life.

Next, I must thank Rabbi Simon Jacobson, who originally suggested this project, and whose knowledge, oversight and perseverance enabled me to complete it.

My thanks also go to:

Uriela Sagiv, my editor and new-found friend, who took my innermost thoughts and feelings and turned them into words that sounded like my words…

Mendel Jacobson, who was there at the beginning (listening and taping) and at the end (researching photos and maps, and organizing all the loose ends)…

David Portal, my son-in-law and attorney, who took the time and effort to make sure the contents of this book accurately reflect the events that took place and portray the persons involved in the proper fashion…

Vivian London, my cousin, who read the manuscript in several different versions, offered her wise advice and urged me onward…

Ruven Ellberger, my nephew, who contributed the title, *Ani Maamin*, "I Believe"…

Philip Orner, who took the time to make many useful suggestions…

Batsheva Lubin, who designed such a fitting cover as well as the book's layout…

Ya'akovah Weber, who did a meticulous job of proofreading…

Finally, I am enormously grateful to my beautiful daughters, Leba, Karen and Chanie, who have brought me so much happiness throughout my life.

And last, but certainly not least, I thank my wonderful, wise wife Myrna, the love of my life, for being there with me every step of the way. It was she who insisted that I write down my memories, and it was she who encouraged me throughout this long and sometimes difficult process. Her enduring, loyal support cannot be described in words. Forever is not long enough to express my gratitude.

May God bless all who contributed to these pages a hundredfold, and may He place this book into the hands of those who most need to hear its message.

Leibel Zisman
March 20, 2011
Purim 5771

AFTERWORD

While this second edition of *I Believe* was being readied for print, Leibel Zisman – my beloved husband – passed away. His leave-taking of this world – on Shabbos morning, June 22, 2013 – was no less dramatic than had been his life, and the months leading up to it were filled with astonishing stranger-than-fiction events that could only have been designed by the hand of Divine Providence.

As Leibel related in the last chapter of this book, from the time he opened up about his war-time experiences, he became totally dedicated to the duty of bearing testimony to the Nazi evil and to the even greater message of the faith of its victims. He accepted nearly every invitation extended to him to speak and, whenever he spoke, he riveted his audiences and left them shaken. He spoke with passion and emotion and almost always broke down in tears, because he did not just relate memories, he relived them in real time.

As word spread that he was a speaker not to be missed, the invitations multiplied … and multiplied … and multiplied. The publication of the first edition of this book brought him to the attention of many, and the release of the award-winning documentary *The Lion of Judah* – which centered on his testimony – made him famous. And Leibel could not turn down all the offers that poured in for him to speak. He believed it was his moral duty, no matter how tired he was, no matter how much it took out of him. And he spoke – at colleges, universities, community centers, synagogues, at Holocaust memorials, on remembrance days. I used to say, "Leibel, don't wear yourself out; you are 82 for heaven's sake." But he would not hear of slowing down.

To Leibel, speaking out was a mission – not just to bear testimony, but to do his utmost to use that testimony to wake up a generation of young Jews, whom he saw as half-asleep, as blithely unaware of what sacrifice his generation had made. When he spoke to young people, when he had gotten their attention, when he had brought them to tears and had them eating out of his hand – because they all would come to love him, they couldn't help it – he would admonish them in no uncertain terms. He would say, his voice trembling, his eyes filled with tears, "If knowing what you know now, if knowing the price paid by these people who died just because they were Jews – if knowing all that, you would throw away your birthright by marrying out, then their sacrifice would have been for nothing. Then you would be spitting on their graves!"

Believe me, no young person who heard him, left unshaken. And they wrote to him of how he changed their lives, how grateful they were. Some committed to putting on *tefillin*, others promised to marry Jewish, others to learn about the Judaism they were ignorant of.

On one occasion, Leibel had been invited to join a JEC/Birthright trip to Israel. It was to be a fun-filled event, with meals around campfires, hikes and other sports activities. Leibel heartily joined in, as was his way. One activity was a ride on a zip-line strung over a valley. The youngsters hesitated; no one wanted to go first. So Leibel went first! Although he was four times the age of the youngest participant, Leibel went first because … what can I say, he was Leibel.

As he zipped from one platform to another with a big grin on his face, he arrived at the end and smacked into an inner tube of a tire. Afterwards, he was black-and-blue and quite a bit sore, but as far as he was concerned it was worth the fun he'd had. But then the soreness did not go away. After two weeks, it was clear that something more was wrong.

An examination revealed that, indeed, something more was wrong. He was diagnosed with a tumor under his right arm.

Leibel's response was one of gratitude. Were it not for the zip-line and the tire, the tumor might not have been diagnosed for several years, by which time it might have metastasized, by which time it might have been too late. But here it was early days, and all treatment options were open.

He had the recommended surgery and follow-up radiation. Afterwards, he threw himself into physiotherapy with his customary zeal, happy to have a new lease on life. Happy he had survived once again.

A year after the surgery, feeling chipper as can be, Leibel was back to his old self. He was thrilled to hear that Yad Vashem wanted to publish a version of his book in Hebrew, and he was making plans to return to Israel on Purim and distribute his book to Israeli soldiers.

But then God called him back. And, in His great mercy and wisdom that is beyond us to understand, He chose to do it in a most unusual way.

On May 23, 2013, Leibel was making a *shivah* call in Brooklyn; when he was leaving, he fell down a few steps. It was so strange that he should fall, because he would always urge others to be careful on stairs, and he made such a point of installing railings in his children's homes. Fortunately, he was not alone when he fell, and he was immediately rushed to the hospital, where I was summoned to hear the horrible diagnosis – that Leibel was almost totally paralyzed.

Naturally, all his children, grandchildren and extended family gathered around him. And, as word got out about what had happened, people started coming to the hospital – in droves. People I had never met before stood sobbing in the hallway, telling me what Leibel meant to them, how he had helped them, given or loaned them money, changed their lives for the better. I was sorry that I had to turn away so many, but as loving as their intentions, Leibel needed to conserve his strength.

It seemed that he was rallying around – though the prognosis was dire – when he contracted an infection and started slipping fast. The doctors forewarned us and so we all gathered around him at the hospital – to spend with him what would be his last Shabbos on this earth.

The God to whom Leibel was so grateful for the many blessings in his life granted him one more blessing. In leaving this world Leibel didn't suffer pain. He didn't suffer a humiliating decline of his mental or physical attributes. He went out with a bang – as he himself would have put it – at the very height of his powers and activity. His family got a chance to say good-bye to him, a chance to express our love for him, and a chance to part from him with love.

And yet, knowing all that, acknowledging the mercy of that, I still feel such a deep sense of loss. I feel such a deep void, and I miss him – I miss him beyond belief – every waking moment.

But I do take comfort in the knowledge that even though his soul has moved on to a better world, his words in this book will continue to serve as his everlasting legacy in this one. I thank you, dear reader, for hearing out his story, for sharing it with others and for taking to heart his message that, despite what we might witness and experience, a loving God is watching over us all. This is what Leibel believed, and this is the testimony of his book – *I Believe.*

Myrna Zisman

IN MEMORIAM

הונצח ע"י הרב התמים

ר' אריה לייב זיסמאן נ"י

לעילוי נשמות

אביו החסיד

ר' שרגא פייוול

בן החסיד ר' דובער הי"ד

אמו הצדקנית

מרת ליבא בלומא

בת החסיד

ר' מנחם מנדל ראסקין הי"ד

אחותו צביה הי"ד

אחיו חיים ישראל הי"ד

ת.נ.צ.ב.ה.

לעילוי נשמות

הרה"ח ר' פנחס מינץ הי"ד

ורעייתו צביה בת הרה"ח ר' מנחם מנדל ראסקין הי"ד

בנותיהם:		בניהם:
סימה בת הרה"ח ר'		לייבל ב"ר פנחס הי"ד
אברהם נפתלי הרץ לוין ע"ה		נח משה ב"ר פנחס הי"ד
חנה בת ר' פנחס הי"ד		שלום בער ב"ר פנחס הי"ד
נחמה בת ר' פנחס ע"ה		גרשון ב"ר פנחס הי"ד
רבקה בת ר' פנחס הי"ד		חיים אברהם ב"ר פנחס הי"ד
מרים בת ר' פנחס הי"ד		
איטה בת ר' פנחס הי"ד		
אסנה בת ר' פנחס הי"ד		
דבשה בת ר' פנחס הי"ד		

הרה"ח ר' אברהם בודנוב הי"ד

ורעייתו מרת רחל לאה בת הרה"ח ר' מנחם מנדל ראסקין הי"ד

בנותיהם:		בניהם:
שרה בת ר' אברהם ע"ה		שמעון ב"ר אברהם הי"ד
אסתר בת ר' אברהם הי"ד		בנימין ב"ר אברהם הי"ד
צביה בת ר' אברהם הי"ד		
מרישה בת ר' אברהם הי"ד		
חיה בת ר' אברהם הי"ד		

הרה"ח ר' יעקב וונגרין הי"ד

ורעייתו מרת ביילא בת הרה"ח ר' דובער הי"ד

בנם הילד ישראל ב"ר יעקב הי"ד

מרת טאנע בת הרה"ח ר' ישראל הי"ד

יבדלו לחיים ארוכים

הרה"ח ר' שלום דובער בן הרה"ח ר' אברהם בודנוב שיחי'

מרת אלה גרינגרס בת הרה"ח ר' אברהם בודנוב שתחי'